Blazing River,

and

Magnificent Military Discipline

A Diary of Twelve Days in China

Annabel Stockman

119 Rotherhithe Street
London SE16 4NF

© Annabel Stockman 2006
1st edition September 2006
ISBN: 9780955384301
ISBN 0 9553843 0 3

*This diary is dedicated to Chung Chung,
Ping Ping, and Hua Hua,
and to all foundlings past, present and future.*

*"Of all things in the world,
people are the most precious."*
Mao Zedong

CONTENTS

INTRODUCTION

In the early nineteen eighties, influenced by a change in US foreign policy, China had begun to open to the west, tentatively and guardedly. Western journalists were sending back reports of the real China, street life China. At that time I saw a television news report in which the narrative described the plight of mothers in the countryside who were bringing their baby girls into cities and abandoning them on the pavement outside main train stations. The film showed tightly bundled babies in bright polyester laid in a row like stranded butterfly cocoons. Commuters' feet walked past the bundles; the babies were so helpless, I remember thinking, that like tipped skittles, they could have rolled out of sight. The report explained that in practice this was a form of family planning; a desperate one given that there is no legal process through which a mother can give up her baby and, as a further contradictory burden, in a situation where it is illegal to abandon your baby. Constricted by the financial penalties (in some cases cruel punishments) on families who produced more than two babies, poor, uneducated country women had few options. The best option for their babies was to risk illegal abandonment in a safe and populated environment where the baby would be found and taken to one of the country's 100,00 'welfare institutions'. In an orphanage a baby might receive an education, and a lucky baby might even be adopted. The worst option for a mother was infanticide.

The cause of this terrible situation was China's one-child policy which was introduced in 1979. There had been a history of disastrous floods and famines which had caused widespread poverty and suffering, particularly in rural areas where thousands starved. The policy, which advocates delayed marriage restricted to producing one child per couple for city dwellers, and two children for rural families, was intended to reduce the growth of a rapidly burgeoning population which was outgrowing its capacity to feed itself. Millions had died of starvation from natural and man-made disasters (in the early nineteen sixties local village cadres had exaggerated their crop production to Communist officials, giving the government over inflated figures).

I

The government had no choice but to implement a policy which opposed traditional attitudes about family expectations. The policy put huge pressure on rural families who clung to the practice of bearing children until a boy is born, often discarding unwanted girls along the way. It was, and still is, a matter of family honour to produce a boy who will carry the family name and provide for his parents in their old age, and it is necessary for families in rural areas to be large enough to work the land to sustain themselves.

While the policy has significantly reduced the population (by about 250 million people) and eliminated the threat of famine, it has also generated many millions of orphans, and they are mostly abandoned baby girls.

I had no understanding of the history or the scale of the problem for these desperate mothers described in the three-minute news report, but I was touched by the crisis for those unseen millions and their families. I visualised the skittles - those bundles of tightly rolled polyester cocooning rolling away from China and dispersing out into families around the world, so redressing the imbalance from nature to nurture. I didn't know then about international adoption; even so I flirted with the notion: how would it be for me to play a part in that?

In 1993 China joined the list of legally designated countries for adoption to the UK. This means that a legal adoption which takes place in China is recognised by the UK as valid. Currently about 7,000 babies a year are legally adopted overseas, about a hundred of them to the UK. In the last few years the Chinese government has softened adoption law in order to make adoption available to Chinese families already with a birth child. These individual efforts make very little impact, however, on population figures which currently stand at a fifth of the entire human race.

I and my husband Olivier became interested in adoption and the power of nurture - as opposed to nature - as an alternative, meaningful way of building our family, and at Easter 1996 we began the lengthy process of an adoption application for a baby girl from China. I was still touched by the notion of thousands of unwanted children on the other side of the world beginning their lives in institutions, often in under-funded places which cared also for elderly people, deaf and blind people, delayed and disfigured people, even illegitimate children. To make a family this way felt fair, equal. As a prospective father Olivier was proud to share the

II

process so evenly, proud to be redressing the balance from 'nature' to 'nurture', and proud that we were not in the business of trying to reproduce ourselves in order to make a family.

We live and work with a group of people in warehouses on the Thames at Rotherhithe in London. As Sands Films and Squirrel Films we make our own films (Little Dorrit, The Fool, As You Like It, all directed by Christine Edzard) and service outside projects, providing costume and prop workshops and offices. At that time we were working on a film directed by Zhang Zheming about young Chinese people living in London. The Chinese crew was from mainland China, Guangdong and Hong Kong. They barely understood each other because Mandarin and Cantonese are different languages. We experienced a strange culture shock on our own ground: the sound recordist who was also an architect, acupuncturist and cook and whose shoes were worn down to flakes, the 'continuity boy' whose name was Second (because he was the second son), the assistant director Henry, who as a matter of style and proof of status ate enormous quantities of food, and Wellington Feng, the producer who chose his name as a boy to inspire himself with British-ness. Confused and seduced, we had got a taste for China.

Our local Social Services adoption department sent our application to the Childlink Adoption Society for processing. We attended introductory talks with six couples and two single women at the society's offices. For six weeks in the evenings we listened to testimonials and stories from adopters and adoptees about their experience of overseas adoption. Many of the descriptions were negative and focused on the inherent problems in crossing cultures. We had not thought too deeply about racism, or loss. A child's loss of birth parents, siblings, birthright, birth country, family history and ancestry, family medical history, ethnic identity, and loss of the right to choose their fate (does anyone?) was explored in role-play. For the adopters loss of freedom was also discussed; of course I dismissed it, understanding only now that having small children around means that one is unlikely to be able to follow the course of an independent thought from start to finish in one attempt.

We were asked to examine these issues in writing and to consider them in relation to ourselves, our marriage, and our own family and life experiences. Some of the questions put to us were challenging and searching; the professionals who were preparing to consider our ability

III

and aptitude for nurturing a child expected complete openness from us. We stayed up late into the night writing at our kitchen table, thinking of our parents, our childhoods, and our old, sad loves gone wrong.

Over a long summer we had eight two-hour meetings with a social worker who went through all these issues with us in more detail. While we handed out ginger cake and tea, Janet wanted to know more. Unexpectedly, she seemed to think that the difficult, painful moments in our lives would actually serve us better to be understanding parents. When Janet had collected enough material she wrote a long appraisal ending with her own positive recommendation of our suitability. She then took her appraisal to the Childlink panel for it then to make a positive or negative recommendation.

At Christmas Janet telephoned, triumphant, to tell us that we had "passed with flying colours". Our application reverted to our local council where the Social Services adoption department approved Childlink's recommendation. Our approved recommendation then passed to the Inspector at the Adoption section of the Department of Health who, in turn, agreed with the recommendation. We celebrated by going out to a restaurant and began there - moving the plates to make way for a little yellow exercise book - to write a diary for our future daughter Chung Chung. Olivier had been calling our unknown baby Chung Chung (pronounced Choong) for some time because he liked its sound. Now we felt it was her name; besides when we looked for it in a dictionary we found that it meant the sound of the strike of a bell, the centre, and China (Zhong). As we toasted ourselves on our success Olivier announced that we would make a short film about our time in China to adopt our daughter.

We were making a 3D narrative version of 'The Nutcracker' for a Canadian company. Olivier produced, Christine directed and designed and I worked on the sets and props. We asked a notary from the City to come to the office to witness us signing all our adoption application documents. These were to be sent by the Department of Health to the China Centre for Adoption Affairs (CCAA) in Beijing for processing. With a red seal and a precise manner, the notary certified Janet's appraisal, Childlink's recommendation, the approvals of our local council and the Department of Health, financial statements, police checks, photographs of us, and a statement promising never to abandon our adopted daughter.

IV

The date, which incorporated his flourished signature, was the twelfth of April 1997: the very day, unknown to us then, that Chung Chung was born.

On the morning of the twentieth of April 1998 we were in Changsha City, Hunan province, waiting for our daughter in the gardens behind the Registration Office for Births, Marriages and Deaths. We waited for her in intense heat for more than three hours. There was talk at the Registration Office that it was a three-hour drive from the orphanage and that her carer had hidden the car keys. We watched groups of Americans and Norwegians float in by coach, collect their tiny, crying babies and clamber back into their seats smiling, and struggling a little with the enormity of new life in their arms. I photographed Olivier filming the waiting; we had waited over two years for this moment and I was grateful, for our idea had grown over time into a strong commitment.

Inside the dark Registration Office, I suddenly felt unsure of myself, and I was unable to take Chung Chung from Zhong Ping, her carer, who wept when she finally handed the baby over to Olivier. But I reminded myself of the hard options for the mothers and babies in China. I tried to think objectively about Chung Chungs' options as an orphan there. On balance, and considering all that we had been told to examine honestly in ourselves, I felt that with us Chung Chung had a greater chance to dream, to aspire and - paradoxically - to be herself.

Amandine Chung Chung Elisebeth Jiang Yan ('Blazing River', her orphanage name) Stockman was exceedingly pretty and much loved at Ping Jiang Welfare Institution. Mr Yu, the Director, explained over supper with Olivier that night in Yue Yang that his mother-in-law had wanted to adopt Chung Chung. Olivier made a good relationship with Mr Yu. The following morning we handed over the fixed US$3,000 donation to the orphanage in dollar bills, took photographs and exchanged presents and addresses, promising to keep in touch.

Back in London it took time for us to settle. Our little, instant family caused a lot of excitement; the notion of Chung Chung as a foundling brought out strong feelings in people. We were quietly observed handling the baby; we were told how to carry her the western way (though she was used to the Chinese way); it was remarked how special she was (this pricked my conscience for removing her from China); we were asked if

V

she slept through the night (this meant little since Chung Chung had learnt not to expect attention during the night); we were asked if her birth parents could be traced. No one, including ourselves, really appreciated how institutionalised she had been, and now, how irrevocably severed she was from her roots. She smiled at everyone, which gave the impression of understanding on her part. She said her first word 'boat' within weeks of her arrival; she seemed to be aware of the need for her to assimilate and integrate. At the park people spoke to us asking if her father was Chinese. I didn't quite know how to answer, so I said 'French'. They smiled politely, uncomprehending, but satisfied in some way by my answer.

We sent photographs of Chung Chung, plump and smiling and some of her first drawings to Zhong Ping and Mr Yu in Ping Jiang. We sent regular money donations on Chung Chung's behalf to her 'first family' as recognition of their good care of her. Mr Yu replied effusively and poetically in small, rushed, handwritten characters. We kept his long letters in a file and in another file we kept the new names and addresses of the other girl babies who had shared Chung Chung's dormitory at Ping Jiang. Olivier communicated with their new families via the Internet. Chung Chungs' contemporaries now lived in Belfast, Boston, Indiana and Massachusetts. I imagined Chung Chung at eighteen meeting up with them to work with the children at Ping Jiang during the summer.

When Chung Chung was two years old we wrote to Mr Yu asking whether he would be able to suggest a suitable brother for her and we began an official application to adopt a healthy child up to a year old of either sex from China. Soon after our application papers had been sent to the CCAA in Beijing Mr Yu wrote to tell us that he had a suitable baby brother for Chung Chung: his name was Jiang Xiao Hu ('Little Tiger River') and apart from a split lip he was in good health.

Mr Yu sent pictures of a baby boy with crossed eyes and a deep hare lip; he was pictured looking into the camera from a high chair sucking his fist and lying on the floor in a yellow summer dress. We were very excited and we replied immediately to Mr Yu that the baby looked adorable and that we would officially request him by name through the CCAA. We sent our request and information about Little Tiger River - we called him Ping Ping, meaning gentle or equal - in the diplomatic bag of the Department of Health's Adoption section.

VI

The CCAA formally 'invited' us to travel to China to adopt Ping Ping. This time Olivier suggested that I write a diary of our adventures of Ping Ping's adoption in China and develop it into a permanent document and companion to Chung Chung's film. We left for China in the middle of a funding crisis for the warehouses and for our children's film, 'The Children's Midsummer Night's Dream'.

This diary is an account of the events and of our experiences on our trip to China to adopt Ping Ping. Unexpectedly we found Ping Ping to be unwell; he was delayed both physically and cognitively. This threw our family into a moral dilemma, one that revealed culturally divergent attitudes about truth, compassion, humanity and the individual...

In sorrow we left Ping Ping to return alone to Ping Jiang while we flew to Hangzhou to adopt a healthy baby boy: fourteen month-old Hua Jijun, or 'Magnificent Military Discipline'.

On our return to London Olivier posted an SOS for Ping Ping on the adoption site on the Internet. Diedre Dudley, an American who had seven other adopted children, responded immediately. Eight months later she collected Ping Ping from Ping Jiang.

I have not dealt with the politics of adoption or those of China herself. The original entries I made at the time are, of course, subjective; they are reproduced here in bold.

During the editing of the diary itself I wrote additional material from memory. This is because as our time in China extended and my experiences became increasingly more intense, I made fewer entries. In their retelling now, however, my memories have been awakened and the events have again become vivid.

There were moments when Olivier saw something that I hadn't, and times when we did things separately. His short entries are set in Italics prefixed by O.

Annabel Stockman
Rotherhithe,
London 2003

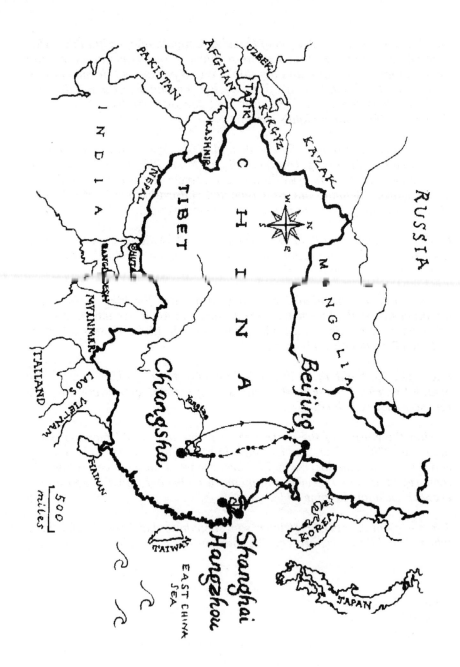

VIII

THE DIARY   2nd March to 29th March 2001

Friday 2nd March 2001, Rotherhithe, London.

The irrepressibly cheerful bird clock twittered seven o'clock, even in the pallid grey darkness of morning on the river Thames. Olivier and Chung Chung (my husband and our three-year-old adopted Chinese daughter) were singing and exchanging on the notions of death or why thunder thunders. The sound of whirring from the blender wafted towards me with the encouraging smell of fresh coffee. In the kitchen father and daughter competed with the radio tuned loudly to a French station. I found a particularly deliciously warm and inviting corner of the bed and drifted...

London was, according to our diary, **'Snowing, cold, wet and dark. Still wintry.'** O (Olivier) was working very hard, too hard at times, to keep the film ('The Children's Midsummer Night's Dream'), the studio, and the buildings by the river Thames on track and solvent, and our little family, happy.

My thoughts turned to Ping Ping or Jiang Xiao Hu (Little Tiger River). He was 'residing', as the Chinese say on their official forms, at Ping Jiang (Gentle River) Welfare Institution, Hunan Province in central China; the same orphanage Chung Chung had been in when we collected her - one year and eight days old - from the Changsha registration office in April 1998. Ping Ping shared Chung Chung's Chinese 'family' name 'Jiang' (River) which was given to all the children at the orphanage.

Chung Chung was born on the twelfth of April 1997 and brought officially to Ping Jiang orphanage on the nineteenth of May. We first saw her in the courtyard gardens at the rear of the registration office in Changsha city. It was the twentieth of April 1998 and fiercely hot and bright. We had been waiting three hours in the heat watching groups of foreign adopters arrive, meet their babies, take photos in the gardens and return to their coaches and move off...The difference in size between some of the women and their diminutive Chinese charges was something to ponder on. I did ponder; for

1

three hours I pondered on the whole adoption process while we waited in the courtyard gardens for our first meeting with our future daughter Chung Chung, known at the orphanage as Jiang Yan or 'Blazing River'.

In the silent stillness of those courtyard gardens at noon when all the workers and householders were absorbed in the serious business of eating, we watched, electrified, as a smartly dressed young woman, in nineteen fifties' tweed jacket and skirt, tight stripey jumper and white winkle pickers, walked around the side of the building towards us. She was carrying a very pretty baby dressed up in a canary yellow nylon suit with pink applique butterflies and gold plastic tassels. We watched intently, wondering...The young woman did not walk towards the tenements backing onto the gardens: instead she walked into the dark, cabbagey, pee and nicotine smelling corridor of the registration office.

A series of fragmentary moments and penetrating images jumbled across our vision while the administrative process took over. Steady throughout was the intense, serious gaze of this charismatic baby, Jiang Yan (Blazing River) in the arms of Zhong Ping, the girl who cared for her.

Jiang Xiao Hu (Little Tiger River) or Ping Ping to us, was born on the sixth of May 2000, and was taken to Ping Jiang Welfare Institution soon afterwards. He was a ten month old Dragon. We knew already that he had had a cleft lip, and from the photographs sent by Yu Yong Gao, the director of Ping Jiang Social Welfare Institution, his harelip now looked very neat after surgery. Unfortunately one eye crossed paths across the other at an acute angle, and this crossing gave Ping Ping a gormless look. He looked terribly sweet all the same, and though the photographs did not record his relative size, this baby appeared to be solidly real.

Something had inspired me to call the adoption section at the Department of Health. I had telephoned them every so often over the last eleven months while the adoption application was being processed in Beijing. "You promise not to tell anybody?...I'm doing your papers now, and you have the little boy you asked for! They're in front of me now... you won't tell anyone will you? They'll be posted tonight, guaranteed next day delivery..."

Swept up in the excitement, Neale (studio manager, general factotum, caterer, plumber, projectionist, tour guide, cook, driver and sorter-out of crises and emergencies), Chung Chung, and I hurled ourselves into the dreary, uninviting afternoon, into the studio van, and into the tired offices at Waterloo. We wanted to collect Ping Ping's 'referral' documents (the official, authorised, stamped-in-triplicate offer of a child for adoption, with medical report and photograph) ourselves. It was snowing hard by the time

2

I ran, splashing into the lobby to collect our authorisation to adopt Ping Ping, while Chung Chung slept in the van and Neale ate her crisps.

It felt extraordinary, significant even, that we had received word from the department about Chung Chung on the tenth of March 1998, almost exactly three years ago. Then, we were required to officially respond to the CCAA (The China Centre of Adoption Affairs) in Beijing to say yes, we would like to accept Chung Chung. Now, three years later, we were sending word back by the diplomatic bag that we wished to collect Ping Ping. Then, with Chung Chung, fate chose our baby; this time we had interfered with the process... this time Mr Yu had told us about a suitable baby and we had officially asked the Chinese authorities for him. We had also bombarded the Director of the CCAA, Guo Sijin, with faxes in English and Chinese reminding him of our eagerness and sense of urgency...This time, part of the waiting was to find out whether the agency had actually read our unsolicited requests, or whether the system was rigidly about files and timing...

I noted in our diary that we would ask Diane (the young business woman who volunteered to teach at the Chinese school that Chung Chung and O were going to on Sunday mornings) to roughly translate the birth and medical details in the referral documents; 'translate' now has an irony that was beyond my sensibilities then, and 'roughly', an even greater irony...

Diary: **'It feels quite surreal that our letters have been read, responded to...by unknown officials, in a formal, pre-determined process. They methodically work through ordinary applications by the hundred every day; we ask something unusual, out of the ordinary, to make them do irregular work; but they do it. They respond. And all this time we have not had a response, until now. We never were truly convinced that, if you ask, you can get. Someone at the CCAA has translated our requests, the letters have been passed on to the relevant file and to the relevant 'document archivist'. If we're lucky and we can travel soon-ish, we'll be in Beijing again in April; Changsha in April, and this time, I'm sure we shall see Ping Jiang Orphanage. I just hope we have a good interpreter!'**

Monday 5th March 2001, Rotherhithe, London

Chung Chung and I drove through another dark, wet afternoon back to the Department of Health in Waterloo to deliver the papers which contained our enthusiastic acceptance of Ping Ping. Downstairs in the lobby we chatted with Christine Manning from the adoption section (she processed overseas adoptions around the world for people whose surnames began L to Z). Chung Chung pretended to be shy, twirling herself in and out of my coat, while Christine and I talked about the mysteries of the Chinese and how they work. Exchanging on the peculiarities of our application we theorised on why Ping Ping's referral only had pictures of him at three months (pre lip-surgery) with no mention of the operation at all! The passport-sized photograph of Ping Ping - who was named in the documents as Jiang Xiao Hu (Little Tiger River) - was at first shocking; the baby, supported from the back by a large, hidden, hand and slumped square-set to the camera as we would imagine a cross sumo to pose, had a thickly gouged, blood-red, open fissure running from a distorted lip up to his left nostril, and eyes crossing into infinity. The flat backdrop to this alarmingly uncompromising photograph of a three-month old baby in a messy drapery of limp flowery vests was of the most Chinese and inexorable and pitiless, luminous blood red.

The ladies at the department were very polite about this unsettling photograph. It was "getting the baby, and caring for him, that mattered..."

The medical report sent to us - and by implication endorsed - by the CCAA, described a cleft lip and palate. In all the letters and faxes we received from Mr Yu, a cleft palate was never mentioned; clearly the CCAA were being over cautious... All our attempts at getting definitive translations of the various letters from Mr Yu through Chinese friends and acquaintances, the headmistress at the Chinese school and enthusiastic booksellers in Chinatown proved hopeless. We were asking Cantonese Chinese people to understand Mandarin Chinese using a written language they shared, but whose spoken language and idioms they didn't; it was like expecting Polish people and Italian people to communicate and it was exasperating at times. Hing Tsang our Chinese filmmaker friend had been getting on well with Mr Yu on the telephone from London, but the conversations merely amounted to exchanges of pleasantries and very little information about the baby emerged. Mr Yu, it seemed, thought it beneath him to discuss the baby with a go-between.

'Yesterday O went to Chinese school with Chung Chung. They all coo-ed and

4

clucked at the photo of Jiang Xiao Hu. 'Dragon boy! Good fortune!', they said, and expressed fury at the mass abandonments. O says that the more he learns about the Chinese language, the more he is mystified, frustrated, bewildered, and excited!

This is roughly how the process has gone to get Ping Ping here.

March 1999. We wrote to Childlink, the adoption agency, to begin a second adoption application.

September 1999. After the homestudy with our social worker, Janet, our application officially to adopt a child of either sex between nought and twelve months from China, is accepted. We are through, apparently, in five minutes. Janet still had to put our case convincingly to the panel, even so.

January 2000. After our confidential file (addressed incorrectly by the adoption section at the Borough of Southwark) goes missing amongst the Christmas post, turns up at an anonymous government office, and is eventually rescued by a conscientious office worker who has opened the file and sent it to the Childlink offices, the London Borough of Southwark finally clear us for overseas adoption.

January 2000. Soon afterwards the DoH Inspector clears us for overseas adoption.

March 31st 2000. Our application dossier arrives at the CCAA offices in Beijing.

March 2nd 2001. The CCAA offer us Ping Ping. We need to wait between four, six or eight weeks for permission from the Chinese authorities to travel to China.

In the meantime Mr Yu has been sending news and photos of Ping Jiang Orphanage and of Ping Ping, and we have been trying to respond since September 2000, but with great difficulty. The orphanage has moved site due to the floods in late 1998, apparently not far, but far enough away for the local postman not to deliver our letters there.'

5

Tuesday 6th March 2001, Rotherhithe, London

'We are dazed and stupefied and excited, hesitantly blinking into the void; the long-anticipated moment we thought we were prepared for arrived today from the CCAA at the DoH. Our permission to travel is here! The offer of Ping Ping came on Friday, the permission to travel to China to collect him came today!

O and I are almost stammering as we try to think of what to arrange; what to take (me), when to time events (O), and the big, big day (us)...and thinking about how Chung Chung can spend her last few days as our only child in splendid, luxurious, un-interrupted singleness!

We talk about holding back the big moment for a few days once we're in China to give Chung Chung a chance to acclimatise and to enjoy a few, last, days as our only, and very special, child. We talk about her being able to prepare herself for Ping Ping's arrival in what is also her birth country... and significant for that. Our visions of an ideal roll and roll...

Opening the rice paper envelope carefully I look again and again at our treasured photographs of Ping Ping. Two are early pictures; he has a fluffy halo of almost blonde hair which matches the lemon mousse girls' dress he's wearing. The harelip is deep, dividing his large, rounded cheeks, and his eyes cross a little. The pictures must have been taken in the summer; they show him lying and propped up on a table in a sunny courtyard. The others must be when he's a little older; again outside, the baby is wearing a thick padded hooded jacket, and he is sitting in a high chair but this time his operation has been done, neatly, and he is bigger and his hair is now dark.

Chung Chung is very excited to go and collect this baby. She looks at the photographs with a thought of her own first photograph at three months old. As she slowly and methodically understands more of her own situation she regards Ping Ping already as a companion, a companion in life, a brother.

I have done lists, O is on the internet looking at flights and we're both imagining similar fantasies... a long meal with Mr Yu, slowly unravelling the histories of both children - through a wonderful guide, who can translate every nuance and inflection - and piecing the beginnings together, for the children's interest when they're older... and for our interest now...Who knows?'

6

Friday 9th March 2001, Rotherhithe, London

I was beginning to visualise the practicalities of being in China, and I considered most particularly the question of public lavatories. The public 'conveniences' I had seen - at least the impressions I had formed of them, mainly from the smell - had not been encouraging. I didn't think Chung Chung would like to crouch at a hole encircled by interested on-lookers.

'We plan to leave on the sixteenth of March by Air France from City Airport to Paris, and after a gentle wander at Charles de Gaulle airport, from there to Beijing. A day in Beijing and the train to Changsha at five p.m. Potty and water with plenty of picnic required. We still have no idea whether the cabin we have booked on the train has a loo in it...we are told that there is a choice of Chinese or western. Yes! But where? In the cabins, or located somewhere in the carriage, or in another carriage? We need a chamber pot! Our diary could be called 'To China with a Chamber Pot' or 'In search of a train with a private lavatory'.

Predicting the weather is, again, not so simple. Everyone has opinions, or no opinion. This is true, in fact, about everything to do with China. When we collected Chung Chung in April 1998, Hunan (if one compares the meridians it is situated slightly north of Bahrain in Saudi Arabia and south of New Orleans, Louisiana, in the Gulf of Mexico) was hot, sweaty and humid. In Yue Yang on the shore of the great Dongting Lake, the air conditioning had been more disagreeable than simply being hot and airless in the hotel room with the window open. Chinese cities are so busy and so loud that to open the window at night means one accepts to accommodate an overwhelming cacophony from the streets with you in your hot and stuffy hotel room. This trip with Chung Chung to collect Ping Ping could possibly be quite cold and wet in Hunan in March.

We're all pale; Chung Chung and I, cold-y, runny-nosey, and irritable with the excitement. Chung Chung by turns crying like a baby or sobbing like a teenager; "You're going to make me cry!..." O still fighting the negative forces outside; still smiling, still apparently able to jump off the mad carousel, switch off and smile and cook a delicious supper. Me, I'm haunted by apprehension...

I love Chung Chung in an indeterminate way, (not measurable, like John Donne's sunne, moone and starres...) we are very similar, we share the same frustrations, and I feel like her adult counterpart sometimes, ungrown...at

7

times she shows something truly real and pure, and I'm stunned, full of admiration, and my love for her is incomparable...

Saturday 10th March 2001, Rotherhithe, London

O's passport was about to expire on the seventeenth of April. This would not do for entry into China, where the authorities expect at least three valid months remaining.

I left my mother at home reading the paper in charge of Chung Chung and dashed to the Passport Office in Petty France after arranging an interview through a very helpful young lady I spoke to on the phone. I had spent the three previous days on the telephone wrongly responding to pre-recorded instructions and impatiently pressing the incorrect buttons.

'The Police were everywhere, vans parked both sides of the street. I asked a young policeman without a helmet (he was approachable I thought because he looked happy) if they were there because of the recent activities of the Real IRA (they had just left a car bomb outside the BBC in White City). No, he said, we're having breakfast before we go off to the football. He looked happy I suppose because he was just going off to have his.

Getting the passport in one morning was painless; I had the relevant form filled in, the correct number of photographs of O, the right money in cash, and a covering letter explaining our rush. I waited forty-five minutes, just time enough to observe the tatty condition of the place, rather like an unemployment office of the late seventies and early eighties; all cloth and plastic uniformly worn down, all paint peeled beyond recognition, a grey, rhythmically speckled band of scuff marks on the walls at scuff and leaning height, an incomprehensible numbering system and the dull-eyed expressions of people who seem to have been waiting permanently underground because they hadn't prepared their papers first. I moved off triumphantly into the open air with a brand new passport for O. It felt like a very positive newness to begin our Chinese adventure with. My success, I felt, was earned. I remembered all those hours of waiting in the days when I too was innocent and unprepared, paralysed by the notion that it could be seen as almost indecent to prepare one's case.

After lunch while O battled upstairs in the office to keep the film, the business and the buildings on course, Chung Chung, my mother, and I pulled out all her (recently re-washed and re-ironed) baby clothes and measured each one according to the description of Ping Ping's length in the medical report from the CCAA. The notion of our Chinese adventure sends my mother cold with anxiety - yet she calls Ping Ping 'a dear little thing'. O very tired, me, another

9

cold and tickly chest already, an echo of the pneumonia in February.'

Monday 12th March 2001, Rotherhithe, London

'Chung Chung and I drove to St Martin's Lane to get the tickets from China Travel Service. We seemed to sail by car to Shaftesbury Avenue in the first clear sun of 2001, arriving across the road from the travel agent in St Martin's Lane by the window of yet another, new, coffee parlour. I left Chung Chung at China Travel in a comfortable seat surrounded by brochures for the Far East and Asia while I went out to move the car to a parking bay. The Chinese girls in the office discreetly eyed her up and down. But in the time it took me to move the car across the road and return to collect our tickets, Chung Chung was surrounded by them all, entertaining them and generally acting the part she felt they most wanted from her. For her pains they gave her delicacies from their packed lunches; pink wafer biscuits and perfumed Chinese sweeties.

Princess Chung Chung is clearly a good luck charm. We secured our tickets surprisingly easily. I asked the girls what the weather would be like in Beijing. They looked surprised and giggled in puppy yelps. They hadn't been to Beijing they said. One, in pink, with long black hair curled into thick ringlets laughed heartily, 'We haven't been to China...ever...!'

We motored calmly on to Portland Place to the Visa Section of the Chinese Embassy. A queue already - a mixture of self-conscious, stiff English and pushy Chinese youths...and a number of innocents busily, some desperately, filling in their forms and asking in high, anxious voices where the nearest passport photograph machine was. Chung Chung behaved beautifully while we waited in one of four queues. She sat on the high-backed chairs flanking one wall underneath a very, very large watercolour of peacocks in a heavy, shiny black frame. An equally square and large-framed Chinese woman in utility trousers and shirt was sitting under the peacocks in what seemed to be a state of meditation; hands on thighs palm up, knees suspended directly over toes, back straight and eyes open but unblinking and directed ahead. She could have been watching the giant screen television on the opposite side of the room, catching the odd glimpse through the fistfuls of paperwork in the queues. The snowstorming TV showed footage from a Chinese satellite channel of the Taliban in Bamian, Afghanistan. They were dashing about excitedly in front of the two biggest Buddhas in the world they were intent on pulverising. It was a sickening sight. No one took any notice except Chung Chung, and possibly the solid woman she sat beside.

After an absorbing and entertaining short wait of twenty minutes the high glass window was ours. The Chinese woman behind the window looked

11

reassuringly sensible and westernised. On tiptoes, and tenterhooks, I handed over our paperwork, including our permission from the CCAA to travel and our three British passports. Chung Chung hovered below, too short to see in at the window. The woman's business-like expression changed suddenly into a warm and excited broad smile."You gar you adatted darta here wid you?"

I lifted Chung Chung up to show her off through the window. Our sensible lady called to the other clerks in Chinese, presumably saying, "Hey everyone, an adopted Chinese girl!" The three clerks at the other three windows (each with queues curling back to the doorway) stopped work and came over to our window to peer at Chung Chung. They waved, clapped, grinned ecstatically and seemed to be dazzled at the sight of a Chinese little girl in the arms of a westerner (who was slowly sinking into the carpet with the weight). Chung Chung was clearly, from their reaction, some kind of exotic rare breed.

The violently over-excited reaction from the clerks in contrast with the lack of expression from the meditating woman was I thought, as we left the packed room, a taste of things to come.

Thursday 15th March 2001, Rotherhithe, London

'We are a little twitchy tonight. It is now ten-thirty p.m. Neale will take us in the minibus to City Airport tomorrow at ten-thirty a.m. My mother will come with us to wave goodbye. Lida at BLAS (The Bridge of Love Adoption Service) has been unable to get us tickets for the return to Beijing from Changsha by train. We shall have to spend an extra night in Changsha, and spend extra on the hotel and the airfare back...'

(BLAS - the Bridge of Love Adoption Service - is a government agency which arranges travel, accommodation and guide interpreters for foreigners for the overseas adoption process in China. Adopters are encouraged to use the official agency because it is linked to the CCAA, the government department which processes the adoption applications.)

'...O is very tired doing the PAYE, last minute financial fire-fighting and counting up our money. Everyone loves the film -so far so good- but what about money to love the film?

We shall see Ping Ping on Sunday afternoon with Mr Yu. We've got follow-on milk and bottles etc - in case. He seems to be quite small...not very, just quite...his head circumference seems small. Sunday seems so near in time looking through London eyes and a lifetime away through the eyes of the stranger who experiences time in China.'

13

Friday 16th March 2001, Aeroplane, London, Frankfurt, Beijing.

'We are now in a jumbo jet (I've never flown in one before) in Business Class, Lufthansa. We are being very well looked after...silver service and white linen napkins; they try to press us with as much alcohol or freshly squeezed juice as we want. The flight attendants are beautiful and intelligent; they are available to tend to our every need but we're too shy to actually demand attention from a flight attendant. We're not experienced travellers like the other occupants in Business Class; we're apologetic and tidy, we don't avail ourselves of the space in the way our neighbours do, nor of the service in the same important manner. This may be because we haven't paid the going rate.

This has come about because through the China Travel Service we booked flights with Air France - an offer so cheap etc...But at London City Airport our little plane to take us to Paris was showing serious signs of not arriving from Paris at all.

In anticipation of an enjoyable trip with Air France I had bought Chung Chung a very good dinosaur book with stickers. We settled in the departure lounge, relishing the comfort of the soft armchairs, the quiet (there was no background music or announcements) and the lack of people. However our contented wait grew into delay and Chung Chung grew more and more impatient that we were not on our way to China. At the Duty Free shop two big bottles of Jamieson whisky were on offer for the price of one ordinary bottle - this in honour of St. Patrick's Day on the 17th. We had no choice; we got them.'

The realisation that our plane was not coming to fetch us hit us suddenly. O and the Air France clerks arranged straightaway for us to fly Lufthansa by little plane to Frankfurt, then on to Beijing also by Lufthansa.The only seats left were in Business Class. We would arrive in Beijing only an hour after our scheduled arrival. We were incredibly lucky: a solitary, tired and cross traveller had been bussed to Heathrow and back again in search of a plane to take him to Paris and he was pacing angrily. I didn't really expect travel difficulties to begin until we got to China. So I was dreamy and full of confidence in O and the smart Air France clerks. I couldn't resist being fascinated by the Lufthansa girls; unlike the trim Air France girls, they were big framed, flat footed and slow. I had plenty of time to observe them while O dealt with Air France, and Chung Chung sat on the counter enjoying his teasing: the unique kind he does when under stress and which he believes will relax everyone else...

14

The little plane from London to Frankfurt was delightful, a proper plane, but the air pressure hurt my ears. By the time we arrived in Frankfurt, I was anxious about more air pressure from another take-off and another landing.

At Frankfurt there were long queues for the Beijing flight. Mostly Germans and Japanese. At the check-in it was scramble time, as though everyone had started before the whistle. An enthusiastic Chinese woman official at the check-in took too long to let us through, instead wanting to indulge Chung Chung; above the noise of the melee I thought she said, 'Does she come from Shanghai?' O thought she said, 'Is she shy?' Both of us glanced meaningfully at the queue and speculated on a polite way of asking an important Chinese official to get on with it.

Business Class on a Jumbo is big and entirely removed from the realities of flying. Air pressure did not, apparently, exist. Chung Chung, knowing that we were, finally, on our way to China, was almost apoplectic with excitement. She climbed, twisted, contorted, spiralled, lounged and sank deeply into the upholstery in a series of acrobatic manoevres in her £3,000 seat. Finally she slept in it, sleeping one of the best night's sleep she's ever had, and she slept and slept and slept, sleeping through our soft landing.

A nota bene about the bathrooms in Business Class on Lufthansa. Naturally, they are very posh and serenely comfortable. There is a notice at the sink which asks that you tidy it after use. I understood that I should re-polish the stainless steel bowl and leave it looking brilliantly shining. I did so ... Beware the laser beam; it operates the cold tap when it senses a human presence in the sink...

Saturday 17th March 2001, St. Patrick's Day Beijing

'We are at the Zhong Min Plaza Hotel, a relatively small building of which the frontage opens onto a corner of the courtyard shared with the CCAA building! For anybody involved in trying to adopt a Chinese baby this would be the most astounding notion; to see the outside of the building where the people who deal with our applications actually work!! Wow!! Our guide from BLAS, Lida (not pronounced Leyda, or Leeda, but L-eye-da) offered us a tour of the CCAA offices!!...Wow!! Without hesitating we said, yes!!!

Lida had not checked with Air France about our delay, consequently she was very agitated by the time we did walk out into the waiting crowd at the newly built Beijing airport, the only westerners with a small Chinese child in a pushchair. It was the pushchair as much as the child which caused the excitement and the engrossed stares because everyone carries their little royalty in their arms in China. Young well-off couples who like to emulate the west use a pushchair as a status thing. (I read in a newspaper article that the Japanese are the most intelligent people because their babies are never put in prams but always carried.)

An air-conditioned people carrier took us along the highway towards the centre of Beijing. O teased Lida, and Chung Chung swivelled coyly and flirtatiously, pretending not to understand any Chinese. When she had had time to collect herself Chung Chung launched into singing her small repertoire of Chinese songs. As we approached the City at speed (the kind of speed in heavy traffic that makes my right foot press down hard on an imaginary brake pedal) it became apparent just how much Beijing had changed since we were there in 1998. Rough, grey little shacks jostled with construction equipment: cement mixers, tarpaulins, wheel barrows, big blocks, and the dust - a thick layer of purple slate-grey sand blown in from Mongolia - on the leafless, well ordered trees and the pagoda-shaped shack roofs. The sand gave the place an eerie thundery glow; everything down a few stops, like an eclipse of the sun.

Our driver ("no spik Ingwish") with a gentle humour in his open, smiling face and his awkward, expressive miming, delivered us to the old-fashioned hotel in the courtyard behind the CCAA offices described as Zhong Min Plaza at no. 7 Baiguang Road, Xuanwu District. Our brief stay there (a long morning until teatime when we caught the train for Changsha) revealed the short-stay version of hotel life. An elegant and simple old-fashioned

16

Government style lobby, very Chinese; polished maple and a Dragon shield emblazoned on the back wall, a modest reception desk with five clocks on the wall behind - Beijing, Rome, Melbourne, Paris, Moscow, but no London. A heavy silence echoing over an imposing floor of hard, near-black granite. Very shiny and slippery and a young woman in the background discreetly polishing it.'

Our room for the day was tobacco-reeking and furiously loud with noise from construction work on a site next door. Our open window brought in a gentle, soft breeze, just like the soft water, but the overpowering noise of building and dismantling, alongside the chattering of town sparrows, broke into any dreamy nostalgia we may have been nurturing from our last visit to Beijing. I became aware in a moment that the net curtains billowing so gracefully at the half open window were filthy...then the floor registered as a series of malign dark stains on an oil-grimed carpet, and the stale presence of tobacco now seemed to cling.

Chung Chung jumped and boinged on and off, from and to, the two single beds. We began to feel odd. (It was half-past three in the morning British time.) O wrestled open one of the bottles of whiskey while I looked for clean glasses. I get into picnic mode very quickly in hotels; the rooms always seem to be enticingly well supplied, but not quite enough...and I feel the urge to be inventive.

We had lunch with Lida at a large and -when we arrived- empty restaurant, the back entrance on the courtyard diagonally across from the hotel. The grand entrance was on the street side. Chung Chung was now scratchy with tiredness. We were feeling dizzy from jet lag; both of us felt we were on a boat, a bobbing, listing, and very big boat. We went for a walk along the Plaza past the CCAA building with a grumpy Chung Chung in a pushchair lent to us by Lida. Again, long hard stares in our direction, in a non-committal kind of way followed by further considered, but non-committal, observation in a continuous cycle. I watched for signs of communication, looks of engagement or recognition between them and us. None took place. Even so, O triumphantly bought a battery for the stills camera from one of the shops which were like stalls at a fairground, but the girls at the counter sold him the battery without comment; they were conspicuously unimpressed by us.

Back at the hotel room - which we now realised was used for daytime assignations and smoky meetings and therefore only the ashtrays were emptied - we optimistically re-packed, arranging all our gear in different places in order of priority and potential...those resonant four p's for the

17

traveller: packing, priority, potential...and peeing. How we are enslaved to our imaginations and our comfort!

The new Beijing train station is monumental, monolithic and strident with big slabs of stone, shouting Fascism, Communism ...big! Bigger than the new airport, recently completed, and weird in its monstrous scale and its aesthetic of German architecture in the 1930's.

A wearying sit with Lida in the VIP lounge. I'm ambivalent about these VIP havens which are a major part of the hierarchy of the workings and frictions of everyday Chinese life. I inwardly reject and refute the notion of anything other than equality - especially when I the foreigner receive special service - however my scruples disappear when I am faced with the conditions: the lack of hygiene and the noise. After a worrying moment with a station porter who kidnapped our luggage for a fee - I thought he was intending to load our luggage onto the goods wagon - we gratefully sank into the black leather chairs and sofa. We immediately could see why this was a resting-place for VIP's; heavily varnished wood, aspidistra plants in pots, and western style separate 'ladies' and 'gents'.

Lida was tired, and seemed to have got tense with the porter. In the VIP lounge she became irritated that I called her Leeda (as in the Swan). I asked her where her name originated. Oh, she was given her English name by a professor who taught her English, she said enthusiastically. "Iss orr name, vay orr; ancien". I became less and less convinced by the wise professor, and more convinced that the professor had meant Liza. I questioned myself also, while O took a grumpy Chung Chung off to the VIP loo, and I sat feeling lost in one of the vast soft leather chairs. Why do I get caught in these circular conversations about things that are so unimportant? Even in China.

'I'm writing now from the luxury and dehydrating heat of our four berth cabin as we go yaggady-yaka, yaggady-yaka from Beijing to Changsha. O is reading Andy Pandy to Chung Chung who is now v. hot, argumentative and beyond overtiredness. Polystyrene pillows, I predict, will have no negative impact on me tonight, and after a little toddy of Jamieson's, and stretching out in the drying heat of a bottom bunk, I'm ready to go yaggady-yaka myself. I watch the view outside sliding past at different speeds as the train by turns hesitates, trips, brakes and accelerates. Low hutongs with grey and purple dusty roofs, heaps of bicycles leaning against heavy plant machinery, from which somebody has hung their washing. Wherever you go in China people hang washing everywhere and anywhere; I wonder, not at the amount of washing, but at the hard-to-get-to places and the frighteningly dangerous

18

places the women in China are prepared to hang washing from. The outer limits of Beijing look grey, luminous, poor, dusty, and in parts cramped and sparse, and all with a steady up and down rhythm of washing like a perpetual stream of bunting.

The cabin door is flung open. I wake up, realising I had been nodding off; the warmth and the comforting thumps and squeals of the train (top speed about 40 miles per hour) are soporific and reassuring. The hoot of the train has a sorrowful tone, a bleak tone, reminiscent of American cross-country trains. A handsome, apparently very young woman in an ultramarine official uniform and important, round, hat tries to take our supper order. Confusion, weak smiles, and apologetic looks all round. We can't communicate at all! We feel stupid. The young woman is not daunted. She departs rapidly, with a positive swish of the cabin door, to get reinforcements. The view outside, through our 'video screen' window, darkens, the darkening landscape rushing on as though we remain still. I help O and myself to another toddy. An old, but freshly laundered white linen cloth covers the little table in front of the window. Dusty orange plastic flowers in a little glass bottle at the window signify the welcome to make the cabin feel like home, and the great thermos full of boiling (or once boiling) water under the little table encourages me to start; we brought instant coffee this time! The thermos draws my attention to the floor, a carpet so grimy it shines like leather... and as I look across the grubby confines of the cabin floor I see odd pairs of sandals under the bunks, and I shudder, imagining all the people who have left them, and not, apparently, noticed'.

I understood later that the Chinese change into slippers once 'at home'; they are uninhibited about this and seem very eager to be 'at home' anywhere.

'The video screen darkens again. We are unwilling to turn the cabin lights on and break the spell. The cabin door is thrown open again, with an unmistakable air of authority, with the air of someone who has a mission. It is Stella, (we learn later) responsible for the smooth running of our carriage, accompanied by an English speaking passenger from the cabin next door. He, again, looks incredibly youthful, and still clutching the deck of cards he was holding during his game, in surprisingly good and clear English translates the menu to us and communicates our requirements to the gloriously beautiful, friendly, and reassuring Stella, 'chef du train' as O described her. Stella is stunning to look at, due partly to her complete, unassuming confidence in herself and her role. In the west we seem to have become neurotically complicated about so little. But then I would feel confident too, if I were in

19

charge of the services on an overnight train and wore a big round official ultramarine blue hat the size of a small bicycle wheel.

They leave, with bows and friendly shakes of hands, and with happy satisfaction. Chung Chung, now in pyjamas, obliges 'in character' as it were, coyly smiling and flirting with these people who are genuinely amazed and curious at our, so to say, 'ethnic mix' and at Chung Chung's extraordinary turn of fate; from Chinese baby orphan to European western child of (presumably rich) loving family.

Looking more closely at the curtains at the window, I hesitate about drawing them, they are dusty and greasy, but more important there is a twinkling planet out there in the prussian blue of the sky we cross below. It seems to be in the east, and it is very bright. It is impressive and it draws me to it, and my imagination would like something to come of it.

Each bunk has a thick duvet rolled up at one end, rather like a roll of hay. When we undo them they bounce into life as irrepressible polyester. To draw them up over one's shoulders is not a snug thing, they bounce off and reflect the dry heat of the cabin. This is not cosy, and in this dry and gritty train heat, my nose dries up and I have a compulsion to clean my teeth, blow my nose, and jump into a shower...all at once.

Our cabin door swishes and thumps open once more. Stella, with support, arrives with our supper: boiling hot noodle soup with a large omelette floating ontop, freshly-steamed cabbage, and hot spicy chicken for O. As in any Chinese restaurant anywhere in the world probably, our little window table is arranged and re-arranged Chinese-style to accommodate all the dishes. We start our grand picnic as soon as is polite, after taking photographs of Stella cuddling Chung Chung. Big smiles and private thoughts all round, in a most polite way. When this happens I have the most surreal feeling, and this question arises: do Chinese people have more moral justification than I do to cuddle and comfort this little Chinese girl, my daughter? Well, do they? Maybe..?'

We hadn't realised that Stella had asked the cook to prepare for us a special supper of the food reserved for the crew. The other passengers were served the standard dishes of the day; dishes which seemed to us to be a great feast of boiling hot, spicy ethnic cooking unknown to us but clearly delicious and good value. We were wrong, apparently, when we heard later that the food on Chinese trains is considered to be dreadful. Nevertheless this meal turned out to be our best and most enjoyable during our short time in China.

The card players next door continued, their cigarette smoke penetrating further and deeper into our cabin, while laughter and activity filled the corridor outside. There was a relaxed, almost party feel to the journey. All the passengers were making an event out of it; an opportunity for serious talk, plenty of laughter, eating, smoking, spitting and betting - with cards and games - and all of these noisy activities enjoyed in soft little slippers.

Through our window the night outside darkened again, the countryside became sparser, with intermittent shocks of scattered smallholdings and dilapidated out-houses leaning against each other for support and held together with washing lines. A new, powerful, sentry light on the apex of the collapsing roof of one dwelling seemed to keep an entire lane of shacks standing semi-upright. Then a slow plunge into the luminous dark again when the rough ground could be seen, just, by moonlight. I watched that planet again, and thought of Ping Ping. Swells of apprehension and impatience rose in me. I was almost too hot, and really too soggy to recognise the scale of our endeavour, and nearing the moment, the eye of the storm, I was divided: I loved the state of suspension we were all in and the excitement now of what was about to be. I loved the imposition that time was making on our journey to Ping Ping. This yaggady-yaka, squealing, braking, slow-moving limbo was a still place to be, a quiet place between the shrill noise of two years of preparation and the anticipated confusion and noise of the first moments of our meeting with Ping Ping. After so long to prepare, I think I felt then, in the train, that I could have remained in this half-way place for some time; I had not really prepared myself for Ping Ping...I hadn't really adjusted to Chung Chung.

I managed - almost didn't - to brush my teeth (in a camping sort of way) and experimented with the western-style lavatory, which formed a flimsy division between the tiny cabin for the crew and the tiny cabin for catering facilities. A man in a hurry came out quickly - I think I had un-nerved him by trying insistently to get in, and wrestling with the door handle. What I saw was a lavatory, yes, but I would need wellington boots to wade across the floor to it. It was not a reassuring sight. I used Chung Chung's potty after that. But Chung Chung, with a perverse twist, decided that she was not prepared to risk an accident with the potty. O agreed to take her to this western - style lavatory at the end of the carriage. Taking Chung Chung to public lavatories abroad is one of his designated jobs.

Cocooned in my hot lower bunk I followed the noises and the rhythms of the train, I watched oddments of buildings and settlements fly past in the moonlight. I began to feel soothed by our repetitive limbo; the cosyness, the now low piped musak, the sound of happy card players, the notion that we were travelling eighteen hours halfway across the country - five hundred miles of bumps and cheerful commotion from Beijing to Changsha - along the ground, yaggady-yaka. I felt hopeful about things as night began to take over. That planet was still there. It was going the same way.

Sunday 18th March Train, Beijing-Changsha

'A very long night for Chung Chung in combination with jet lag; strange, unexpected hungers are happening, apparently independent of us, as though our food-mechanism hasn't noticed that we are now hours out of shift. Chung Chung has woken at six a.m. Chinese time, eaten a rice and chocolate bar and flopped back down into O's lower bunk opposite mine. After beginning the journey playing musical beds they ended up sleeping on the same bunk, O in his clothes, watch on wrist and teeth un-brushed, Chung Chung in her pyjamas, bed-washed, teeth-brushed and story-read.'

O and I sat on our low bunks leaning on the little table at the video-window and watching the sun rise over Hunan. The window showed a restless panorama of wet, green endeavour; an infinite labour of patchwork in small plots of worked land, broken by shapeless, random patches of scrabbly, unworkable, wild places.

'People are up and working early, sporadically in ones and twos at first. The morning outside seems to be fresh and dewy, overhung by the misty blue-grey of dawn. Occasionally a munching, still figure of a white or honey-coloured water buffalo can be seen half-hidden in the irregular scraps of green. We will have to wake Chung Chung up to see the oxen at work so early.'

The red earth of Hunan Province began ribboning and swirling past, dancing up and down, in and out, reminding me of the absurd and self-important Leslie, our young guide when we were here in 1998 to collect Chung Chung. (His lecture on the red earth peculiar to Hunan which is used for making bricks and tiles was the only interesting thing he had to tell us from his tourist guide patter). And now suddenly the landscape opened to a flat, grey, watery expanse stretching out to infinity under the low morning mist. We guessed that we were approaching Dongting Lake and Yueyang - places that, for us, hold memories of high drama, strong emotion and an exhausted, dehydrated and bewildered one year-old Chung Chung.

Yueyang was the place, also, where I had risked a sweeping generalisation about the Chinese: that wherever you go in China there are multitudes of people everywhere, and that wherever they are, there will be someone squatting over a little stove making tea, and always in outlandish places; balancing on a girder on a building site, perched high on top of a rice bale carried by boat on a lake, hunched low over a fire while another washes her long hair in a bucket on the pavement of a city street, where three make-

23

shift 'walls' improvise as a bedroom, and passers-by unwittingly become voyeurs...

'China is waking up inside and outside. In the smoker's cabin next door one of the men has lit his first cigarette of the day; the fresh smoke weaves its way into our cabin and he is clearing the phlegm from his throat Chinese-style. Now I understand why all public places have spittoons placed in strategic places: in stairwells, at the end of escalators, at lifts, by doorways; and why TB is so common in China...

'Past more and more shambolic buildings and shacks squeezed in-between the patchworks, places that look uninhabitable...dirty, torn cloths hanging at open, frameless windows, and yet always, lines of washing... More and more eccentric home-made buildings speed past, until the tenements begin. A frisson of agitation falls across our fellow travellers; we are arriving in Changsha. I fall in with the spirit of the tension of arrival and I start to re-pack our gear in an order I think will help when we come to un-pack. This is not easy when a night of train travel has left everything and all of us dried up, grubby and in complete disorder. The noise of excited agitation has reached fever-pitch.'

We were out of the train and on the platform, carried up in the tidal wave of Chinese disgorging en masse. Our 'exit' system worked very well given that not one of the passengers or guards offered help. While O fought against the flow to get back onto the train to collect the last of our luggage, Chung Chung and I stood on the teeming platform blinking into the dark. A mini people-carrier drove – squealing - across the covered platform ignoring the hordes dragging luggage, and arrived alongside the carriage door and beside us. A large-framed, unusually tall Chinese VIP, a star of some sort, emerged from the train in a white jumpsuit; an apparition. Darth Vader instantly sprang to mind. I was surprised to see him bend down and squeeze himself into the back of the van, minded by two short stocky men in the usual colours worn by Chinese men who aspire to business: pond-brown, grey, and green, worn down to a non-colour from excessive use. Our delightful, beautiful Stella hovered close by, probably to check that the VIP was happy. This VIP thing in China, this apparent devotion to status, grates on me.

We exchanged addresses with Stella in a state of genuine optimism. I really wanted to ask her why, when she commuted between Changsha and Beijing three times a week, she chose to live in Changsha amongst the tenements where the risks of fire are so high and the expectations of life are so low.

24

The shrill noise on the platform began to penetrate sharply and jet-lag began to drag me down by the shoulders. A small, thin, wiry man grabbed hold of our bags insistently, determined to play porter. Stella sent him away and we gratefully, apprehensively, moved off and down a covered slope towards the ticket barrier. I had the craziest thought when I saw the massed silhouette of people waiting: I hoped our guide would recognise us...

The crowd at the barrier was heaving; an excited, teeming grey thicket of intense, rigid faces. No smiles or embraces, mostly jostles and shouts. Jessie was holding a card with 'Stockman' written thickly in black, the 'S' twice the size of the 'N' which nearly slid off the edge of the card. We approached her smiling, with relief mostly. Jessie was tall, slender, pale, her crooked teeth noticeable when she tried, against habit, to return our smiles.

Jessie rushed us through the crowds at the station as though we were celebrities with a plane to catch. It is not easy to manoevre a child in a buggy, drag two huge suitcases on wheels, with plastic carrier bags of duty free, potty gear and food hung painfully from spare fingers, and keep pace with an anxious guide who runs off to a waiting van. All this into a torrent of commuters moving, monumentally, against you. For the stranger to Chinese ways the first lesson is learned at train stations; push or be pushed.

O: 'We left the platform and found ourselves in the crowd queueing for the little booths where officials checked the passengers' tickets. From then on it seemed that the crowd was stationary and infinite. A crowd had formed on the other side of the booths too and the mass seemed permanent both inside and outside the station. Once in our little van we were driven through a mixed crowd of pedestrians and vehicles.

No individual can stand out in a crowd such as this, yet outside the station I noticed a man whose face had been marked for life with the tattoo of a Chinese character in broad sweeps of magenta. This was not a decorative tattoo; it described the crime he had committed. I was deeply shocked. The man was walking with an old woman, maybe his mother, and they struggled to cross the roundabout. He looked worn out and broken. He was free, I thought, but to carry the stigma of his past must be a permanent humiliation. I was frightened by the brutality of this archaic punishment and I kept silent; I did not want Annabel or Chung Chung to see this.'

25

At nine a.m. on Sunday morning at the grand fountain outside Changsha train station the strollers were already out, meeting at the fountain and strolling off arm in arm, girls with girls and boys with boys. The pollution of the city was beginning to heat up in the sun, the stall shops had been trading for some hours, traffic was crawling and the orchestrated hooting of cars and buses was underway. I was reminded here - watching, mesmerized, through a soporific haze the frenetic activity through the window of our own little people-carrier (courtesy of UNICEF) - that I had formed another generalisation about the Chinese. They appear never to sleep.

In spite of the sharp morning sun the city looked grey, grisly even, and bleak; all its edges were badly worn and chipped. The people looked poor, uniformly poor.

The Hotel Hunan Furama was situated near the station and opposite a huge building of shopping halls on a very busy, pot-holed two-way street. There was a smooth concrete space raised up off the street for 'set downs' outside the glass swing doors of the hotel, but once on the street itself you could fall down a hole instantly if you weren't looking at the pavement. My memories of the streets of Changsha now are distilled into the terrifying images of the cars and bicycles approaching us determinedly head-on and of the 'pavements' and their unpredictable dangers which lurked in them.

The hotel has a formidable set of grand glass entrance doors which swing, revolve, or refuse to open at all, and with them three or four mostly redundant young men in swing-door uniforms and pill box hats who gaze at foreigners in stupefaction. This hotel has the status symbol of all hotel status symbols: a massive, intricately patterned, polished marble floor in the entrance lobby which has to be kept permanently polished by a girl in polisher's uniform.

We landed at the hotel check-in desk in an euphoric but dishevelled state. We were going to meet Ping Ping that afternoon. Very, very pretty girls stood in smart uniforms like flight attendants, behind a tall desk which ran almost the depth of the lobby. O provided the information they needed about us with Jessie, while Chung Chung and I slid, slipped and tapped about on the polished floor. Jessie looked pale, tired and worn, and with her bad teeth and badly drawn eyebrows, she did not seem happy, and certainly not as optimistic and enthusiastic as Lida was.

All the girls - even Lida in a subtle way - plucked the outer halves, the 'tails' of their eyebrows, and substituted hand-drawn ones in what looked like thick brown wax crayon. This looked strange; eyebrows made half of black hair and half of a brown wax line. (Not quite so strange, though, as the shopkeeper of a little general store in Paris whose creepiness crept up on me when we were 'just looking'... it was O who first noticed - he's taller than I am - that the shopkeeper had painted his bald head with thick black lines of wax crayon, to re-instate, presumably, the hair he had once had.) The eyebrows of the young women we met fascinated me, and I studied them, even at moments of crisis. It happens to me generally when I cannot understand a language that I take refuge in visual meditations like this: in China there is so much to absorb from all sides that at times it is overpowering.

Jessie came up with us in the lift to the second floor - I'm not relaxed in lifts - while the bellboy struggled with our luggage. When he finally appeared his hat was askew and he was single-handedly pushing and carrying all our cases, with the carrier bag of potty stuff hanging from his teeth. I'm embarrassed about the idea that hotel staff actually wait on you. I love hotels and especially setting up home in them but the sight of this boy struggling and compromising his pride in his uniform bothered me; he was unintelligent and uneducated and pride in his uniform seemed to be the only thing he had. He wasn't management material. He hovered a long time waiting for a tip until Jessie told him to leave. We didn't have any Chinese money ready. If he'd come back on a false errand later we would have tipped him, and made friends with him.

We asked Lida later during our return to Beijing why it was that the majority of people we saw working in the service industries - hotels, stations, trains, shops, restaurants - were young women? Lida painted a picture of the men: heavyweight business executives, high-flying, on-the-up, future managers and executives, who all worked (in smoke-filled rooms I imagined) behind closed doors. They were so important that no one saw them. Therefore, she explained, the young men one would see working in the public domain were in a humiliating job, because, she implied, they were stupid. All the (mostly) young women we dealt with were as sharp as razors. She was right about the young men we met though; they all seemed to me to be dim.

The room was designed as classic Intercontinental style but softened by Chinese eccentricities. Two beds with enormously heavy tapestry patterned bedspreads which smelled of cigarettes; an impossible-to-open tinted double-glazed picture window which looked onto a street which never sleeps; a standard lamp which got in the way and you couldn't turn on anyway; an oversized TV which was unmovable; and a desk which contained the goodies: the list of telephone extensions for the laundry, room service, the business bureau, sewing repair kits; and giant paper towelling slippers. The Chinese are an hospitable people and the hotel rooms demonstrate this aspect of their character to the tiniest detail. The room instructions in English translation: *"In order to Appreciate yourselves the Satisfactory services don't Smoke in the Bed"* are always a delight to me. The mini bar is lit seductively by a down-lighter on the way to the bathroom, and below this is the practical shelf with cups, packets of green jasmine tea, and the well-worn thermos of once boiling, now hot-ish, water.

Chung Chung began to boing between the beds. Jessie lingered while we inspected. We were very hungry, very grubby, and now, very excited to see Ping Ping. Jessie was in touch with Mr Yu by 'phone. He had two other babies with him. He would take them to their new families first and then come on to us at the hotel. He would be with us by about four o'clock that afternoon.

I switched into home-making mode, unpacking our gear in an order which seemed to be illogical and shambolic, even to me in my distracted state; walking round two huge suitcases to take one toothbrush into the bathroom, organising the baby gear three different ways and in three different places after moving all the movable furniture, and swapping relevant plugs and switches irrelevantly, at least twice. Chung Chung and O shared a bath while I struggled to be practical. O came out of the bathroom complaining of a strong leaning sensation in the bathroom, and a strange bouncing in the bath. We put it down to the dizzying, bobbing jet-lag of plane and train we were both feeling; the disconcerting physical sensation of continuum and momentum which stays with you after you have got off, still spinning.

Breakfast in the breakfast bar adjoining the lobby. A girl maitre d'hotel stood at the door anxious to collect our breakfast voucher. She had the 'maitre d' uniform: a badly tailored shiny waistcoat with a black full length skirt slit to the thigh, and - most fascinating for me - what seemed to be thick, pale brown support hose which fell in generous folds around the knee and ankle. I wondered at this sight as I handed her my voucher and cast around for Chung Chung and O. I observed a breakfast scenario which I didn't think we could ever quite get used to.

We sat amongst the 'shiny shoes' (O's description of the aspiring Chinese male in hard, western shoes) with their mobile phones, and thick acrylic jumpers under their cheap suits. When business talk heated up, so did they, and the layers began to come off while more and more cigarettes were puffed heavily, more fish heads were washed down with a noisy slurp of green tea, followed by a huge burp while reaching for another cigarette. It wasn't easy; the waiters stood at attention inches away from us and the 'shiny shoes' who occupied the surrounding tables all watched us in an uncomfortably invasive, unselfconscious and remote way. Part self-service and part table service, where the waiters are sorely tempted to feed you if you don't appear to know how to do it yourself. Our coffee wasn't and my toast wasn't either. Still hungry, we didn't stay to investigate the business buffet on offer: fish heads, sour pickled eggs, congee, a foul smelling vegetable compote, and beans which looked like our own, reliable, and comforting baked beans, but when I later tried them with a nostalgic anticipation, they were as hard as pebbles. The cultural divide is not easy to reconcile when you're hungry.

Ever since I had yo-yoed helplessly in a lift in the Royal Albion Hotel in Brighton when I was five I've been apprehensive about lifts, and sometimes, unless I'm highly motivated, I can imagine that I'm feeling claustrophobic; I often play out the emergency and pull the doors apart with my bare hands. Fortunately we were only on the second floor, so when O and Chung Chung set off into the wilds of the city for Ping Ping supplies and interesting things, (anticipating a refreshing bath) I was happy - and proud of myself - to go up in the lift alone and let myself into our room with the smart card key. This device to get in was also a challenge in itself for me since it also turned the electricity on.

The room had been newly made up, and an extra mattress had been put on the floor with an enormously puffy duvet for Chung Chung. Two thermoses of freshly boiled water had been brought in and more bathroom *"requisities* [sic] *for your enjoyment"* were set out on the faux marble vanity top: toothbrushes, toothpaste, shower caps, combs, cotton buds, soap and, of course, throwaway slippers, all wrapped in paper boxes and pouches decorated with Chinese characters and exotic dragons. This is Wendy house playing in the grand style.

But I too had a weird experience in the bathroom. I lowered myself into the bath which was disconcertingly below floor level. Rather than luxuriating in a deep, bubble-filled, warm and relaxing float, I became aware that my head was spinning, faster and faster; I felt as though I had stepped onto a boat in a choppy sea. I got out before I felt any sicker, and stood dripping in a fluffy bathrobe... and I still felt sea-sick, my brains bobbing about like gulls on a swaying sea. I staggered out of the bathroom and sat heavily on the end of one of the beds. Our duty free called me like a siren mermaid from its hiding place in the clothes cupboard and a lid-full of Irish sent the sea on its way.

Encouraged and enlivened by my emergency snifter, I got dressed and made a deeper study of the hotel services. I had found the extension number for room service and the system for the laundry service (I was looking forward to the Chinese laundry service) when Chung Chung and O came back empty-handed, and O looked pale. I wondered if he was hungry, or weak from the strange jet-lag we were feeling. He couldn't really say much with Chung Chung there, but he muttered something to me about the stalls in the hall being dreary, being disappointed to find nothing fun to buy and the sensation that Chung Chung and O had caused by being together.

O: 'Maybe we had idealised Changsha; our 1998 trip had been such a great success. Besides, Changsha was the only city outside Beijing with which we could claim some kind of familiarity. I was very keen to return to the Friendship Store in Changsha where we had bought Chung Chung's first toys and where I had found some fine woolen cloth; I had taken it back to our costume workshops in Rotherhithe with a sense of triumph.

Armed with a small map of the city, Chung Chung and I prepared for a long walk. Maps are not easy to find in China and ours was simply an outline of the main thoroughfare, and it was not to scale. I was nervous about the huge amount of traffic, the noisy hooting, and the apparent lack of traffic lights; whenever we crossed a street I carried Chung Chung in my arms. We were both very happy to be out and walking. Chung Chung counted all the dragons she could see, but the surrounding cityscape began to depress me.

In fact I knew nothing of this city. It is vast; nearly six million people live in Changsha and what Chung Chung and I saw of it was very ugly. It seemed that we were in an out-of-date city centre, now redundant, and in need of redevelopment. It was run-down and dirty. I realised that we were too far from the Friendship Store to walk there now.

A very old lady walked towards us on the wide pavement. She had with her a little girl of five or six years old. They were both poorly wrapped up in layers of quilted cotton. The old lady approached us and spoke to us in Chinese. Of course I could not understand her. She became insistent and pointed at Chung Chung, rubbing her thumbs against her fingers: the universal sign for 'money'. The old lady then lifted the little girl at her side and seemed to be signifying to me that she was offering the child to me for money. This made me very uneasy, and I was worried about how Chung Chung would interpret all this. I expressed our polite good-byes as clearly as I could and we set off back to the safety of the hotel. We walked on through smaller streets, but now I was less confident. Obviously it is not a common sight to see a white European male walking with a four-year-old Chinese

30

girl in the back streets of Changsha; people were looking at us hard. We returned to the hotel with no purchases this time.'

We didn't venture out to eat. This was unusual for us, but O was sufficiently discomforted by this unpleasant outing to propose that we should have an unadventurous lunch in the hotel.

The food in the lobby restaurant was much the same as anywhere, but the dishes were memorable for the galvanic activity their position on the table provoked; Chinese waiters (in the case of the Fatherland waiters are mostly young women) have a single-minded pre-occupation with the lay-out of the table. They never ask if you are enjoying the meal, rather, with fixed smiles they remove plates before you are finished, restlessly shuffling and re-shuffling the teapot, the cups, the dishes and the chopsticks. I drew the line at having my napkin thrown open under my chin and manhandled onto my lap; I fought back, holding onto it silently, and determinedly. The thin, pockmarked girl with a wide smile and the now familiar flesh-colour hose which folded around her ankles, let go; eventually.

The girls stood in a circle around us, watching every movement we made and every mouthful we took. They looked longingly in Chung Chung's direction, like children do, waiting for their friend to come and play. It was so disconcerting that I couldn't enjoy the food or observe the surroundings. I tried to imagine how it was going to work with Chung Chung and baby Ping Ping at a table with us; a boy - a boy! - a star turn, how dazzling, how curious, how arresting, how ... exercising..!

Chung Chung slid off her high-backed chair and walked over to the fish tanks. She flirted there with the restaurant staff for some time. The girls seemed to be genuine in their indulgence of Chung Chung. She peered through the glass at the little grass-green soft-backed turtles, she leant down into a tank and stroked the backs of the toads, she swayed in front of the bank of aquaria in which lurked (temporarily) sad, pale lobsters, prawns, crabs, sea bass and eels and other less beautiful, and even sadder, sea creatures.

The waitresses made a big fuss of Chung Chung; they tried to ask us how and why she was with us when she was clearly Chinese and we were westerners... I mused on the predicament of the young women living in the impoverished, ignorant, and feudal countryside in China, and the babies they make and cannot keep. This cruel situation, a situation that has existed for one reason or another for thousands of years in China, caused me to brood. The poison made from the one child policy, poverty, ignorance, the despising of women and the admiration and the striving for

31

the male heir, and a fundamental disrespect for life, causes anguish and suffering to millions of young women and babies and their families. The devaluation of the individual pervading all levels of life is a burden on the entire country; the economy; the politics; the culture; and China's reputation abroad. Yet there were people we met in China who were apparently unaware of the existence of these millions of orphaned and abandoned babies, nor of the events which flow to and from this painful situation.

To the stranger China seems to be a place of contradictions at every turn, at every thought.

After lunch we wandered round the tourist shop in the hotel. No delightfully cheerful, garish paper things in Chinese red and pink: instead, absurdly expensive western imports swathed in the sickly grey-green glow of strip lighting. Who could afford a week's wages for a pair of boxer shorts and who would be likely to want Calvin Klein boxer shorts in Changsha? Someone high up, a 'shiny shoes', must have had an optimistic expectation of the kind of money the average tourist would be prepared to pay for gratuitously expensive things they can buy at home cheaper. Besides, foreign visitors with big money are hardly likely to stay in the neighbourhood around the mainline train station. We asked the smiling lady in twin-set and pearls for a map of Hunan. She searched energetically in drawers under a display cabinet of overpriced Johnnie Walker whiskey. She excitedly brought out a small map of the hotels and shopping malls of Changsha. We left, walking with our backs to the exit, smiling politely. She seemed to understand too late that we were looking for little things, keepsakes, souvenirs... little bright paper things for Chung Chung and Ping Ping to keep.

O needed local currency (in addition to our US $3000 for our 'donation' to Mr Yu) to pay for the registration and notarisation of Ping Ping's adoption tomorrow at the Registration office. The bank in the hotel was the antithesis of the tourist shop in every way. The impression was that we had walked onto a film set of Sheriff's cells in a nineteen forties' American western except that the people behind the bars were not cowboys but Chinese bank clerks. They were drinking large quantities of green tea from multi-coloured thermos bottles, and smoking with impressive intensity while their fingers threw beads around an abacus and counted bank notes in a blur of awesome speed. No smiling here, just figures. And counting. And a chalky dust on unused surfaces. And sawdust on the floor.

Back in our room, the telephone rang. It was Jessie to tell us that Mr Yu would meet us in the lobby in half an hour and that she would meet up with us just before. O was pale, Chung Chung boinged between the beds and my adrenaline shoved me into a higher gear. I tripped on a small step into the bathroom and saw the edge of the basin approach me fast. From the corner of my eye I saw a small drain in the floor and immediately all became clear. It was not so much jet-lag which was making us bob about in there, it was that the bathroom floor was on a very steep incline, an incline from four angles in order to drain the water away.

Downstairs in the lobby the pretty floor polisher was on duty, performing her slow, repetitive, dreamy, solo dance. The scale of the lobby was impressive, flanked on one side by the beautiful girls with their beautifully half-drawn eyebrows and on the other by islands of intimately, conversationally positioned seating arrangements, some in the Louis XIV style, others from The World of Leather. Hovering in silhouette by the bank of glass doors, the well-meaning, but hopelessly slow-witted, young men in ill-fitting bellboy uniforms waited for something to happen.

The notion of handing over a little baby here, in a hotel lobby seemed to me to be a violation, a terrible and cheap thing to do. But this is how it had been arranged, and we had no part in the plans, except to be told when and where... I was very anxious to see Mr Yu with the baby, very anxious to end the waiting for us and for the baby. I felt the strain and tension in me tightening into a knot. The brutal contradictions, the paradox in this situation, like all others in China was hard for me to reconcile. I so easily become irritable and impatient because of my incapacity to bear an unresolved, and an unresolvable, contradiction.

O and Chung Chung skated and twirled on the polished marble. They were, I thought, rather more nervous than exuberant. My nervous energy made me pace. I paced twice up and down the length of the splendid floor, and all the time I wanted to stand outside and watch for Mr Yu and baby Ping Ping. Each time I approached the glass doors the boys became animated, three of them at once opened three doors and all of them smiled and bowed in a way that suggested they were not busy enough. My inner knot tightened. I made signs to say that I was waiting for someone. I was already pre-empting the impact of their long, unthinking scrutiny on us all when our very public meeting finally took place. Even so, I found myself playing the laser beam game. When the boys felt my approach was at a critical distance from the doors, they all opened a door for me, either a swing or a swivel with a great show of speed and efficiency. One of them felt sufficiently brave to practice his English on me, and with a sickly grin he intoned - like men often did who passed us by in the street - 'Ehlorrr!'

I diverted to the corner of the lobby where the wall continued in glass.

33

Searching through layers of net curtain I could see the hotel car park. Out of nowhere appeared the unmistakable figure of Mr Yu weaving through the cars, alone. He saw me wave. I was elated to see him. I smiled. He smiled at me. I felt so, so happy, and grateful even, that he recognised me.

The bellboys were not ready for me this time. I escaped through a swivel door before they had time to blink. I felt myself catapulting towards Mr Yu, my head spinning and swelling with distraction, and I was suddenly aware of the gritty quality in the air, the smell of greyness, and the damp from rain which doesn't wash anything away and remains in puddles. We shook hands enthusiastically, as old friends; lots of smiling, genuine smiling, but a heavy feeling at the same time of a third presence: the ever-present, insurmountable lack of a common language. I had signalled wildly to O and Chung Chung as I flew through the door, and they now joined us outside. Mr Yu was very pleased to see Chung Chung. She looked so pretty, so happy, so bright. It must have been a strange meeting for Chung Chung out there on the forecourt, greeting like an old friend the man who had signed her over to us. It is a frozen moment in my memory of fragmented, excited delirium; hand shaking, smiling, and Chung Chung by turns diving under our arms or prancing and jigging...broken, after some minutes, by the late arrival of Jessie in the Unicef van.

Moving off slowly we returned to our positions in the lobby. Mr Yu and Jessie fell into deep and - interestingly to us - businesslike conversation, with a parity, a correspondence of rank and a lack of deference to the 'superior' which does not happen in the west. By contrast I have seen overt 'kow-towing' by the Chinese, but it is clearly symbolic and it is not felt genuinely at all. In the west we seem to be much more influenced by hierarchy because we privately believe in it, and so feel it deeply.

It wasn't easy to break in, but when O asked where baby Ping Ping was, it emerged, bit by bit, that he was with someone else who we were now waiting for. They didn't tell us who that "someone else" was, of course, but I supposed they assumed we knew what they knew. We waited in the lobby for about ten minutes while Mr Yu admired Chung Chung's "beauty and good health." Then the glass doors opened and flashed, reflecting the daylight outside and the lights inside. Two women walked towards us, one holding a large chrysalis shaped bundle in yellow padding. It was Ping Ping in the arms of Zhong Ping, the same young woman in high heels and a tweed skirt who had carried Chung Chung as a mother carries her baby. Zhong Ping this time had grown rougher looking, she now had glasses and she wore jeans and a thick jacket. I felt a stab of sadness that she was no longer so pretty and that she had not dressed up, nevertheless my sentimental, nostalgic attitude to destiny was immensely satisfied by this circularity, this neat replay of events; my spirits began to soar.

It was difficult to see Ping Ping, partly because he was hidden inside an immense quantity of layers and also because Mr Yu, his wife - who had walked in with Zhong Ping - and Jessie knew each other from other adoptions and had formed a circle around the baby. This and their familiarity with the system and their common language made an unintentional, but effective, barrier. O stood beside Jessie quietly, and as she talked to Mr Yu and his wife, O watched Ping Ping taking in events. Chung Chung and I skirted round the circle bobbing up and down, in and out, to try to see. There was also the unspoken (and still unresolved) question which hovered over the proceedings; at what moment does the 'hand-over' take place? Here, for the second time my ambivalence was exposed; I was not entirely confident about my own role, or my status, at this critical moment in the process. So I felt unable to demand a place, and unable to break into the conversation. At the same time I longed to see Ping Ping.

When Zhong Ping had carried Chung Chung, she had kept her close for as long as possible. She wept to let the baby go when the separation was forced upon her by expediency. We were in our parked taxi asking Zhong Ping about the baby while we waited for Mr Yu's driver to return from his lunch and lead our driver to Yue Yang. She looked at baby Chung Chung wistfully as she described the orphanage routine. Eventually she had to get out of the car and leave the baby with us for the three-hour drive to notarise Chung Chung's adoption. The separation from Chung Chung was too much for her; she wept to leave the baby she was so fond of.

I often wonder whether it is that *how* we manifest ourselves influences the process more than we realise. Or it could be that we are merely passive players in an entirely neutral procedure...

With quiet understatement Mr Yu presented Chung Chung with two large rag-doll white mice, one in a wet-look plastic jacket and trousers, the other in a wet-look dress. She knew they were presents from Ping Jiang, and - impressively for her age - she made polite and cheerful expressions of delight. I could see that she found them creepy. I did, too.

Fussing and smiling and talking and miming and understanding very little we adjourned to the privacy of our room. The room looked too small to accommodate such a monumental event, and with so many of us in there...

In one short meeting Chung Chung was to be introduced to the man we described as her 'first father', the young woman who had cared for her during her first year of life, and the ten month old baby she was already calling 'brother'...we had much to ask Mr Yu and Zhong Ping about Chung Chung as well as Ping Ping. The situation demanded a lot from us; we were to take over the care of Ping Ping and throughout - experiencing tremendous pressure from our expectations, the excitement and the confusion - we needed to hold on tight to Chung Chung.

It began to feel chaotic. Zhong Ping sat down with Ping Ping on her lap facing outwards. She watched Chung Chung trying to play with the large mice, fascinated by her and smiling. Zhong Ping remarked on how "grown-up and beautiful Chung Chung had become". Jessie was translating pleasantries and politenesses mixed with facts and figures; two loud conversations were happening at once, with a third gestured and mimed. Chung Chung's excitement began to spill over... O caught Jessie's attention long enough to ask her to order tea for us from room service. Mr Yu presented us with a framed print of cherry blossomed branches with the legend 'The World Becomes So Beautiful Because Of Your Love' with a small photograph of him, his wife and their little boy sitting on grass in front of a well-appointed apartment block. Our meeting began to feel like a crowded family reunion.

Mrs Yu sat on one of the beds smiling. Unlike her husband she understood English quite well and spoke a little. She had deep red varnish on her toenails and new black platform shoes. I was very struck by her shoes because platforms were absolutely *the* shoe worn in the west in March 2001. Her auburn-dyed hair was permed into waves and curls and her eyebrows were spectacular; each one a long, extravagant, sure-handed sweep of the wax crayon à la Rita Hayworth.

We presented Mr Yu with our own rather eccentric present for the orphanage: rag dolls in bags begun years ago for Romanian orphans by our 'Monday night ladies' at the studio. He was bewildered by them, having never seen anything handmade from the west. O tried to explain that they were made by a group of women connected with our local church. The now familiar clouding of the eyes and expressionless expression drifted across their faces. It was my turn to mutter to O to "leave it...forget it..."

The hard facts emerged in a rush from Zhong Ping. Holding on tight to the large yellow chrysalis, she described an ordered and rather grown-up routine for Ping Ping: up between six and seven a.m., breakfast at eight a.m.: rice and milk, lunch at noon: noodles and vegetables and milk, supper at six p.m.: rice or noodles and meat and milk, bedtime with milk at ten p.m. Two sleeps morning and afternoon for an hour and a half.

O asked Jessie to find out about Ping Ping's hearing. Mr Yu had written to us to say that he had been put under observation for a possible hearing problem. A pause while Mr Yu, his wife and Zhong Ping listened to Jessie translate. Then, as one, they made a cacophony; shouting, clapping, hooting. They laughed indulgently when, at length, Ping Ping turned round slowly, trying to locate the source of the noise. Any specific answer was lost in the hubbub.

And then a small plastic envelope of tiny round white tablets appeared from somewhere. Jessie interpreted for Mr Yu hurriedly; the tablets were "for baby who has been under the weather for twenty days, possibly baby is teething, with bad tummy ache. Cut into three pieces, one piece three times a day."

Above the noise and excitement O asked Mr Yu, through Jessie, if any more operations were needed on Ping Ping's mouth. Mr Yu said "No". I looked at Ping Ping who was listing sideways on Zhong Ping's lap in his (I now noticed) dirty nylon babysuit. I didn't believe he was eating meat; Zhong Ping had proudly said this about Chung Chung who had certainly not eaten meat, or vegetables, mashed or otherwise. I looked at him. He was only ten months old but he was noticeably little. Quiet. Unusually unfussed and content. His harelip was tidily repaired. His unfocused squint, his soggy posture and above all, his quietness were a little disconcerting. I remembered the difficult car journey we had made with Chung Chung to Yue Yang from Changsha to catch the Notary before her office closed. Heat, noise, exhaust fumes and rough road for three hours. Ping Ping had experienced his first car journey that morning from Ping Jiang which was also three hours away on the same potholed major route. Poor baby, I thought, no wonder he's quiet after that kind of excitement.

Greetings, presents and information exchanged, our crowd stood up and moved towards the door for the departure, and thus, the moment of Ping Ping's handover. Zhong Ping handed Ping Ping to O and we walked slowly and noisily, waving and smiling as we approached the lift to see them off. I was still very keen on a visit for Chung Chung to Ping Jiang Orphanage. I felt she was sufficiently clear about her relationship with Ping Jiang and secure about her own position with us that we should try to take the opportunity for a return visit to her "first family" now. Mr Yu smiled warmly and said he'd be very happy for us to visit, but he needed to get permission from the CCAA first. We left it at that, thinking also that Monday was registration day and we would be feeling very happy and high; after registration we would take Mr Yu out for lunch before he drove back to Ping Jiang.

Chung Chung and I carefully peeled layers of tired and un-washed clothes off Ping Ping, each layer thinner, hotter, sweatier and more handed-down. I would rather have left him to decompress gradually in the security of their familiarity and smell, but the clothes smelled very bad, he seemed to be uncomfortable... Ping Ping was small and dirty. He had never been naked, clearly, and he bleated about it, in pathetic little cries. The clothes we had brought with us were too big for him, even though the new ones were for age six to nine months. Chung Chung and I tried to wash him lightly with damp tissues. He bleated even more. We put a nappy on him with difficulty and dressed him in some of Chung Chung's first, hardly used, clothes. Ping Ping remained flat on his back on the bed and after staring at the wall, fell into a fitful doze.

'O and Chung Chung are in the bath together. We had a very rice-y room service supper spread over the bed. Ping Ping was too tired to drink tonight, but we managed to give him a third of a tablet. I lost three of them as they skidded around, resisting the blunt knife. I can't imagine what they are really for. They're not synthetic chemicals; they feel more like processed herbs, possibly a natural opiate.

Baby Ping Ping has a very pretty smile and he is sensitive about stuff being done to his face. There is a thick, encrusted sore behind both ears. He must be very tired from his long day; he is still asleep. His quiet sleeping dominates the room. His littleness has a big presence.'

Monday 19th March 2001, Hotel Hunan Furama, Changsha

'A difficult night. Chung Chung wakeful, needing an unscheduled pee and reassurance. O asleep only at the start of the night; anxious awake, worrying about Ping Ping and us the rest of the night. Ping Ping, next to me, also awake all night, eyes open but not looking or registering and stone still. Me, deep, but fitful sleeps, overcome by the relief that we have Ping Ping with us, finally, but much regular waking, aware of Ping Ping by my side not moving, silent and wakeful.'

At six a.m. Ping Ping was hungry; he bleated with a new tone. O prepared the bottle at our makeshift formula mixing table next to the TV. Ping Ping's gulps and swallows were haphazard; the milk travelled everywhere in large splashes and spills. He must have been used to a different kind of bottle; maybe he was drinking from a cup? We tried that, too, but it was no good. We would ask Mr Yu today what kind of bottles they use in the orphanage. After soaking three small towels from the bathroom with warm formula milk and drinking only part of a bottle's worth himself, Ping Ping fell asleep on his back where we lay him down on the bed, now with eyes shut. Ping Ping was not mobile in any way, nor able to turn himself over, and he certainly could not draw himself up to a sitting position. But then, I reasoned to myself, he's only ten months and he has spent all those ten months in institutional care; he's had a hare lip which made eating and drinking difficult; he's not quite himself at the moment Mr Yu says; and he's had a gruelling journey. In addition to all of that he must be frightened to be with strangers.

'O still suffering sick anxiety as he does from time to time, and severe lack of sleep. Chung Chung completely asleep in a big, soft mound of duvets on the mattress on the floor. Baby Ping Ping also fast asleep now surrounded by soft mounds of duvet in case he turns over. A peaceful, slow morning.'

O looked again behind Ping Ping's ears; he realised that the encrustation was deposit of the dribble which rolled down over the ample baby cheeks and rested there. This conjured up a picture of a baby who had been lying on his back all the time, and a baby who did not get washed behind the ears. While he slept I put some zinc cream behind each ear - not knowing really what to do - and visualised lots of baths and splashings to soften them up.

We had arranged to meet Jessie in the lobby at nine-thirty a.m. to go off in the Unicef van to meet Mr Yu at the Registration office. After the registration and our official adoption of Ping Ping was done, in buoyant mood we were going to celebrate by taking Mr Yu, his wife and Zhong Ping if she hadn't gone back to Ping Jiang, out to a big Chinese lunch. I was going to explain the phrase "slap-up lunch" to Mr Yu.

Chung Chung and O were already at a table downstairs in the breakfast area used mainly by the 'shiny shoes' businessmen. I was fascinated, helplessly drawn to the manners and social aspirations of the shiny shoes. But this time they didn't pay us the slightest attention; they were too busy laughing, smoking, spitting, eating and shouting into their mobile phones to be interested in a western family with a Chinese child, or even two. It was the hotel staff, the waiters and waitresses who have so little to do who watched us intently at close range. Although I had anticipated this, I still found the situation very difficult. I could hardly bear the scrutiny as I walked in carrying Ping Ping.

Chung Chung was not hungry (it was twelve midnight for us) and she began to feel self-conscious, knowing that a large, inexpressive audience was watching her. The audience was very attentive, too attentive, it was claustrophobic and uncomfortable for us.

I became impatient with this very quickly, and left my cold breakfast un-eaten. I took the baby into the stale darkness of a nearby lounge which served as a saloon bar in the evenings. Ping Ping yawned. In the darkness, a shaft of the low morning light which shone from a small, far, window illuminated the cavern of the baby's mouth. I felt drunk, or drugged, as I struggled to understand what I had seen. It was as though I had seen a fairytale dragon or an alien, or a newly discovered species. But what I had seen was a symmetrical, and very deep, cleft palate. I could scarcely believe what I saw and yet it instantly made sense. I thought of Mr Yu, and I became agitated, angry, disappointed, resigned. I looked for a new, further resolve in myself; we would sort this out when we got home.

We talked, briefly, in the foyer while we waited for Jessie who was consistently late. She had a three-year-old daughter who was cared for by the grandmother while Jessie worked as an adoption guide at Number One Changsha Welfare Institution. We tried not to alert Chung Chung to our anxiety. So we talked on practical lines and in level tones. We agreed that Ping Ping's hare lip looked very good, but we couldn't understand why his palate had not been operated on also. We couldn't understand why Mr Yu had said that Ping Ping did not need any more operations on his mouth. We needed to know what the tiny white pills were actually prescribed for. We agreed that we could certainly get good surgery for Ping Ping's cleft palate in London or Bristol, and that we could organise the same for his eyes. However we would have to consider very hard, for Chung Chung's sake, if we discovered other, more serious health complications with this baby. We told Jessie our news when she arrived.

On our way to the Registration Office in the Unicef van I blindly watched busy, damp, grey Changsha ride past on its collective bicycle. Ping Ping slumped on my lap. He didn't perch or nestle, or snuggle or curl up; he slumped in my arms and I trembled as dread invaded my body further, and deeper. I speculated chaotically, trying to understand what was the matter with Ping Ping. I sketched out scene after scene with different endings. O and I were in shock. Jessie looked uncomfortable.

I was falling in love with Ping Ping fast; this baby who seemed to be falling away from us, falling more and more into a drugged state... perhaps the pills, I wondered.

'The registration office is in an entirely different building, in another part of town; where, I have no idea. I lost my general composure early on this morning... A new seven storey purpose-built block comprising - apart from a view of Changsha, an Adoption Registration office which occupies an entire floor and which incorporates all mod cons such as Disney characters dancing across the walls, interpreters, photographic studios for the official family portraits and dictionaries. The ultimate convenience for the harassed adopter is a four star hotel on the two top floors. Americans prefer five star apparently, so I suppose this hotel accommodates the British, the Spanish, the Danes, the Dutch...

The Director of the whole enterprise is the registrar from the old, darkly oderous office in 1998 from where we collected Chung Chung hot and wide-eyed. He had waited through his lunchbreak in his gloomy and dank file-filled office for Chung Chung's arrival. He had taken time over our formalities, (throughout the process I remember we were all silhouetted in semi darkness) and it felt as though he had been extremely sympathetic, attentive, even interested. Now his elevated importance is obvious, even in a foreign language, and he clearly enjoys it as he puffs, benevolently, on his cigarette. In China smoking is not an 'issue', nor is smoking near babies and children. While men smoke all the time and everywhere, women don't do it at all. He smiles indulgently and surveys the foreigners as we are drawn into the endlessly repetitive processings of the formalities in office after office. He smokes, looms over the proceedings in all the rooms, watches the anxieties and satisfyings of procedures with amusement, and practises his English on me. I tell him that we remember him from three years ago. He smiles; the

41

non-committal smile suggesting that he might, then again, might not remember us.'

Mr Yu was waiting for us in the large teak-panelled reception room where an American group had just settled. They had been steered into the building by Leslie, our guide during our visit to collect Chung Chung. Still the same tense, fixed smile, expressing foolishness with every gesture, he was wearing a suit, the very thing for an aspiring 'shiny shoes'. "Leslie!" I called "What a smart shiny suit!" He looked nervous; he probably didn't remember us. Then again, he might have done.

It was here that the Disney characters pranced joylessly across the walls. But then I was disconcerted not to be to retracing our steps to that stale, cramped office with files stacked on the floor to waist height. The Chinese babies belonging to this group of Americans looked to me as though suspended in a cultural and emotional vacuum, neither east nor west providing any immediate, meaningful reassurance. The Americans - they wore large badges of their babies' referral photographs - were focused on 'issues' of bonding and ethnicity: American ethnicity. All the babies sat looking shell-shocked on the laps of strangers. Some of them wore absurd be-ribboned white lace bonnets with oversized peaks. These were Chinese babies, I reflected, babies whose ancestors may have invented the iron plough, the wheelbarrow, the suspension bridge, the spinning wheel, paper, printing, silk, lacquer, the first compasses, matches, chess, the umbrella, and a place for zero in mathematics.

I judged myself, too, and I felt a stab of conscience about my own part in this situation.

The large, cheerfully loud women sat round a huge, polished teak table filling in the first of the endless forms. Their mostly thinner husbands sat on hard chairs lining the sides of the room, the babies, stupefied and silent, sitting upon their laps. I wondered what kind of a night they had had together, these babies and their new parents. I pictured a large group meal in the hotel, where the parents had continued to bond and the babies had yelled.

It is only the British, it seems, who tackle the system of adopting alone; most countries send their adopters out to China together in groups. While travelling to China they bond as expectant parents and they travel around China together on their collective mission. They stay together in the same hotels and together follow the itinerary of a shared guide. They adopt their babies in one session, and go through the legalities, notarisations and visa applications together. They shop, eat and sight-see together; the parents

42

and babies become a cohesive group whose experience and memories become shared and fused together.

A small, wiry official wearing a knitted tank top called out instructions in very good English to the women; it was a collective form-filling rather like Bingo. The man in the tank top called out the questions mechanically, 'performing' his role as both warm-up and linkman. Every so often one of the women would respond enthusiastically, looking very pleased with herself; she had remembered to bring an important document and she could now fill in her form, sure of the right answer.

Mr Yu was sitting in a corner smoking, looking distracted, even distant. We made our greetings without the help of Jessie who had vanished on some errand. We sat with Mr Yu in the corner and I absorbed the bondings of the American group, with Ping Ping on my lap, supporting him with both arms round the baby pouch. Mr Yu and O began trying to communicate with each other. Mr Yu had been learning English from the Internet. He looked for something to write on. O found an envelope in his pocket. Mr Yu wrote on it in English "How do you feel about this?' O returned the question, writing on the envelope: "How do *you* feel about this?' Mr Yu then wrote a small list in Chinese, neatly numbered one, two and three. Jessie returned at that moment. Smiling and in cordial mood we asked her to translate what Mr Yu had written. She mumbled vaguely about a problem at birth.

With no time to ask Jessie to explain, we were called in to the first room for the first stage of the process. Surrounded by noisy officials, men and women, we were swept along by requests to show proof of good character and employment, to sign papers which were stamped each time in triplicate by three different officials, to explain in writing our desire to adopt Ping Ping, and last, while a young man pressed Ping Ping's foot onto an ink pad to take a footprint, to swear on oath never to abandon or forsake him.

In the last room of the process, where we signed our declaration (the last of many signatures) Jessie produced a large Chinese English Dictionary. She was holding the envelope that O and Mr Yu had been writing on. She had written on it also, and she showed us the envelope, pointing to her translation. She explained that Ping Ping had become unwell twenty days before our arrival and that the orphanage doctor suspected one of three conditions to be the cause. She had written:
1. Epilepsy
2. Brain haemorrhage at birth
3. Lack of calcium

This was sudden, and wretched. Except for the very last stage in the process (the taking of the family photo for their records) we had finalised the adoption. Ping Ping was now our baby.

I felt hot, frightened and ambushed. Jessie had known this about Ping Ping from our meeting the night before, but she had not, for one reason or another, chosen to tell us.

O had justifiably suffered apprehensions and forbodings all night. We were both now feeling very, very tired, sickened with confusion and dread. We felt disappointed, duped, and compromised... We believed, even so, that we could, and would, deal with this. I reasoned privately that we had to - out of duty, out of a sense of what is right, just, and fair.

At the same time Ping Ping was diminishing; his presence became less and less palpable; he was now lighter and smaller in my arms, slumped and unresponsive. His retraction, his diminishing was frightening and heartbreaking. In my arms he was becoming less. My instinct to protect and nurture this little baby was at full blast and I was horrified at this diminishing, at his lack of revival in our care and in my arms.

Chung Chung became hot, and irritable; the super-efficient heating system and the lack of fresh air overwhelmed her. She felt the tension in us. She insisted on having her picture taken with us and Ping Ping. A large woman in uniform spat roundly and loudly into a spittoon by our feet. We smiled weakly into the camera, helpless and stunned.

The whole adoption process had taken only two hours; so different from the three-hour car chase back in 1998 to catch the Notary in Yue Yang. Then we flew through the air along the rough terrain which was the only artery from Changsha to Yue Yang. We chased Mr Yu's four wheel drive, dodging the oxen which roamed placidly across the route, avoiding old people and cripples who shook their sticks at us when we missed killing them by inches.

Now we parted company with Mr Yu at the lift, in no mood for a slap-up lunch with him. My feelings skidded with incomprehension and a sense that we had been betrayed, and Ping Ping exploited. Jessie remained with us in the lift, silent, looking down at the floor. We returned wearily to the Hotel Furama through soft drizzle in the Unicef van, not, as we had imagined in a state of triumph, but exhausted. We brooded silently on our momentous commitment.

44

In the hotel room, left alone now, we had no wish to celebrate. A growing, gnawing, fear had appeared amongst us.

'Ping Ping is asleep on the bed, tired out from this morning's ordeal. Changsha looks bleak and grisly. It rains onto the poor, broken people and the poor, broken buildings, and onto the poor, broken roads.'

O called Jessie on her mobile to arrange a meeting. He tried to explain that we wanted to discuss with her the three possible medical problems in more detail. She was due to deliver three identical adoption papers which would have been stamped at the Registration office with the final stamp after their lunch.

When Jessie came up to the room in the afternoon Ping Ping was still asleep. Chung Chung stood by the bed, watching him. Jessie saw at once that we were shocked. She went over to Ping Ping and watched him for a while too as he slept, for once, deeply. She knew there was something seriously wrong with this baby; she herself was a mother and she had experience of orphans by the hundred. She also knew more from Mr Yu and his wife than she had told us. I felt our vulnerability acutely. I was aware now, more than at any time, of the tyranny of the Chinese language. We were relying on Jessie to be our interpreter and our guide through the intricacies of Chinese thought and behaviour. Of course we had found ourselves under her tyranny, too, under her own conditioning to conform, and especially not to lose face - what a tyranny that is to the Chinese psyche! I wrote in a bad temper later that night:

'All our 'information' is via a stagnant, constipated, unrelenting language which is betrayed by a perverse 'translation', founded on a vain pride which refuses to acknowledge the truth for fear of humiliation.'

We sat on the twin beds by the telephone, papers strewn everywhere. I asked Jessie what had happened to our question to Mr Yu about any further need for operations on Ping Ping's mouth. I asked her also whether Mr Yu and his wife had said anything more about Ping Ping's health other than that he was "under the weather"? Jessie answered without any apparent discomfort that she had not translated for us properly on Sunday night. Jessie explained that Mrs Yu, a doctor, had said that she thought Ping Ping's condition was serious and that he could have any one of the three problems they went on to describe, but which, we now knew, Jessie had not passed on to us. Maybe the much-mentioned orphanage doctor was actually Mrs Yu... Confusion or conspiracy? I asked Jessie why she hadn't translated to us everything she had heard the night before from Mr

Yu and his wife. " I don wan lose face an' tell truth hurts." she said, flatly, and perhaps a little regretfully. We saw for ourselves that "loss of face" is a collectively understood shame in China; I had my own opinions about it at that moment. Jessie called Mr Yu on his mobile. His response was to suggest that we take Ping Ping to hospital for a proper check-up.

We looked together at Ping Ping's medical information in the Notary's adoption papers. In the margin titled "oral cavity" the handwritten remark in Chinese described it as "normal". In fact every remark in each column of Ping Ping's health record was the same: normal. Actually this did not reconcile with the medical report from the CCAA, which did, in fact, describe a cleft palate, and which we ignored, assuming wrongly that we knew better because Mr Yu would have been entirely honest with us.

O felt that a hospital check-up was in fact the right thing to do: the actual state of Ping Ping's health needed to be established in order for him to receive appropriate care. The realisation that we may have to return him to Ping Jiang, based on a negative diagnosis, took form between us; having officially adopted Ping Ping, we would have to cancel, undo all this, dissolve our intention into vapour. Un-adopt him. Of course patient, calm Chung Chung would have to take part in this un-doing, too.

'A second very uncomfortable night. O pale, very tired. Me, terribly cold, shaking, and still shaking in a hot bath. Shaking so much that my jaws spring open and shut, causing my teeth to slam together with dull crashes. Chung Chung has become very fond of Ping Ping, I suppose because he is so very passive, baby-like and un-threatening. She is very sensitive to the atmosphere and the strain. She is being amazingly well-behaved, so good. In between our long debates on the whys, ifs, wherefores, hows, she announces that she wants to keep him. O is realistic; he was immediately worried by Ping Ping's look - not the crossed eyes - the look, the vacant, lost, benign, unreachable look. The smile that wasn't a smile. I didn't, couldn't see it; I didn't want to. Now I am terrified that if I can't walk away from him I will be committing us all to great, life-changing difficulties, and for a reason that I don't know...I suppose I feel it is my duty to submit to the situation. Does that mean all of us, too? Ping Ping is the sweetest of sweetest babies, but he does not, cannot reach into our world. O reasons that we cannot submit the three of us to his world; to Ping Ping. Commitment and submission locked in battle. My head is sick from the conflict. Can I justify submission as commitment and nurture, knowing that we owe Chung Chung these things, that we owe her a companion, an equal, not a responsibility?'

We telephoned home to London, weeping down the line at midnight to

46

people settling down to tea-time eight hours back.

We spent the rest of the long night fretting in wretched despair as we played musical beds between the four of us. Any sleep we got was fitful and wrung from exhaustion. Ping Ping, again, didn't sleep, but remained still, on his back staring blankly at the dark ceiling. His stillness was more than alarming; for me it was an agony.

Tuesday 20th March 2001, Hotel Hunan Furama, Changsha

In the morning Chung Chung and I struggled with the overpowering service in the breakfast area downstairs. O and Jessie had left very early with Ping Ping for the hospital for a thorough check-up as Mr Yu had suggested. I had a fight with the self-service toaster to make what I thought was, or should be, toast. The thing was obviously in-built with an incapacity to toast; I tried the same two slices half a dozen times. The stuff remained white and shapeless but scorched palely at the edges.

Leaving Chung Chung to the mercy of the too-attentive waiters hovering at our table, I had to go into the main room and skirt round the central oval-shaped breakfast bar; the choice for Chung Chung was congee (a foul-smelling rice porridge cooked for days), fish heads, beans (the red pebbles), noodles, rice, rice dumplings, hard boiled eggs in hot spicy sauce, chicken feet etc. I chose noodles and Chung Chung worked through them bravely while four young waiters, leaning against a shelving unit for napkins, plates, condiments and ashtrays, watched her intently and unblinkingly.

Chung Chung and I went out for a walk along the main street; it was wet, with fetid, stale, puddles lurking in the pavement cracks, and, unlike the hotel, it was crowded. The interior of the hotel throbbed with efficient harmony; the girls on the desk, the boys on the door, the floor polisher, the low muzak, but immediately outside we were confronted by Changsha life. The looks, the attitudes, the little shivers at our existence, the sideways glances at our material presence... I was aware also of our 'invisibility'; we were cancelled out - registered but unseen.

We were struck by the poverty and by the hard level of existence for the people we saw; Chung Chung was extremely uncomfortable during our short walk. She was conscious of a disparity. The level of existence was shocking, yet we did not really see 'deprivation' as such, more a material, and demoralising poisoning from greyness, brokenness and lack.

We ventured round the corner picking our way through broken, loose stones, rubbish, puddles and a continuous stream of cyclists and pedestrians moving against us. Another long, wide street, equally run-down despite signs of feverish human occupation in the rows of stall fronts. An hotel, abandoned, fallen dirty and chipped, with unwashed windows and broken, hanging awnings was clearly used for gambling and prostitution. It had that stale daytime smell of frenetic night-time activity. Even a pair of splendid white lions on the forecourt had a bleak look about

48

them. Next, a hairdresser's, on whose narrow window were taped sun-bleached collages of all the new western styles stuck onto Chinese faces, and in the back, a small, dark, room with men talking loudly. Then a food shop, also displaying brushes, baskets, and rag mops. Sitting amongst these on the uneven, wide pavement, were three generations of women from one little family. They were not actually doing anything, or even talking together; they were just there amongst the multicoloured mops made of torn rags. A few feet away a man was sending long bamboo sticks down a drain. The smell was sickening. The small family watched mildly as he brought out filth and mire of indescribable type, and left it in dripping clumps on the pavement.

The little family showed signs of interest when they saw us. Grandmother stood, her knees supporting her body, as though she were about to perform Tai Chi. She had a look of history about her; the real history of life lived under repeated incarnations of hardship. She wore tired and tattered blue trousers and jacket, and her short grey hair was held back from her face with a hairclip; I smiled at her and she smiled back. She looked very happy when we turned to walk towards them. Chung Chung and I tried to smile warmly; we found it difficult and we must have looked very unsure of ourselves. The young, squarely-built mother was permed and buttoned-up tightly in a traditional quilted, flowery and much-washed, faded jacket. The little girl looked like a balloon with a moveable head. She couldn't move inside the stiff layers of thick quilting. She sat motionless on a low bamboo stool while the mother and grandmother stood close: they had to; if she had fallen off she would have been unable to get up by herself. She tried to wriggle off when she saw us approach but she was so restricted in her movement that her mother had to stand her on the ground to walk. From her walking I assumed that she must be very little, eighteen months old and only staggering maybe; when they held up three fingers to tell me the girl was three I was shocked: Chung Chung was still technically three - four in a few weeks. (O's theory that the children in China appear well behaved because they are exhausted from the heat and incapacitated by the restriction of the clothing was probably right in this case.) We smiled and exchanged on something, I'm not quite sure exactly what, but on a level that made the moment bittersweet for us, and memorable. It felt that it must have been so for the little family, too, but differently I suppose.

This was very different from the Changsha O and I had enjoyed so much the night before we collected Chung Chung. On our last night together we had strolled along another wide busy street, un-hurriedly looking around us as we chose a restaurant for supper. There was a group of smiling young men sitting on their small motor scooters flirting with giggling girls with long shiny hair. In the darkening light the shops with open fronts were still

49

open. The stacks of buckets, bowls, brooms and brushes illuminated by single bulbs was a cheerful sight. The shopkeepers watched us stroll past. Some smiled. A girl with a long plait was selling sweet cakes on her candle-lit stall by the kerb. At supper a fly dropped heavily and died in our sour-smelling supper of durian soup which the waitresses had recommended. They had also recommended snake. When we mimed polite refusal by pulling faces they all laughed. We walked slowly back to the hotel along the wide, unlit pavements in the dark. Families from the countryside were publicly preparing for bed in improvised shelters on the streets. The long-plaited cake-seller was still there on the pavement in the dark cooking by candlelight. Impressions are powerful things and - paradoxically - so dependent on our state.

Chung Chung and I arrived back in the lobby assuming that we were in advance of O and Jessie. The girl-polisher was in her polisher's uniform as usual, pushing, as usual, her wide floor polisher up and down the huge lobby floor, back and forth continuously, all day, and slowly like an automated lawn mower.

We chanced upon Jessie who was hurrying out of the hotel. I was surprised when she told us that O and Ping Ping were upstairs in the room already. She told us the news. The doctor at the hospital had confirmed that Ping Ping had Cerebral Palsy and she had recommended that he be admitted immediately. Jessie was about to call Mr Yu. They had already been to the Registration Office to cancel the adoption with the Director. This important man, who had chatted to me so personably on Monday - and who expected us not to forsake our new baby - cancelled the adoption on Tuesday. He had called Mr Yu on the telephone himself instructing him to collect the baby.

Chung Chung and I stumbled into the lift. What about our promise never to abandon the baby, our baby? I visualised O and Ping Ping up in the room, miserable together now the reality of our situation was worse than we had imagined. The lift seemed to take an age to get to our floor. What about the legal process, I thought frantically. How can the legal, notarised adoption be reversed in one procedure? And on the instructions of one person? And after all that legality and stamping? Babies mean nothing here, it seemed to me at that moment, as I waited impatiently for the lift doors to open and to run to our room to see O and Ping Ping.

O: 'Jessie was waiting for me in the lobby at eight a.m. The drive in the Unicef van took us a long way through the grey city. I held on tight to Ping Ping; I was very frightened. We drove through steep, narrow, winding streets; streets which felt *strangely European. At a conjunction of five streets the van pulled up by the railings of a large, old, grey building. It was terribly run-down and looked as though it had never been maintained. The windows were un-glazed, protected only by rotten shutters. The building was set back behind a small ornamental garden in the centre of which was a bronze statue of a young dancing girl. It seemed so much like a Catholic mission building in Central America that I almost expected to see nuns walking about.*

Carrying Ping Ping I followed Jessie into a large, noisy hall filled with anxious, elderly grandparents holding very young, crying children. It was not easy to see the babies and children because - as usual - they were hidden under many layers of clothing. We were required to register Ping Ping to qualify him for a five yuan (fifty pence) consultation with a doctor. Jessie dealt with this while I watched over her shoulder, aware that I (a male westerner carrying a very unwell Chinese baby) was being watched too. We were handed a little exercise book with Ping Ping's details hand-written on the front cover and a stamped receipt for the cost of the consultation.

At the entrance to a busy corridor crowded with more waiting people were two women dressed in white sitting behind a table. One of the women collected Ping Ping's exercise book and filed it in a shoebox with many other little books. The other woman filed the receipt in another shoebox. I sat down on a bench in the corridor and waited with Ping Ping in my arms while Jessie talked to others waiting. People collected by the open doorways in the corridor which led into doorless consultation rooms. Visitors and nurses and doctors in white walked up and down the corridor which also led directly to the wards. As a consultation room became free a nurse would collect an exercise book from the shoebox and call out a name and a room number. I watched a frail grandmother with a crying little girl. They were not city-dwellers and must have come in from the countryside... I began to realise that many of the people in the hall had spent the night on the hard benches.

Jessie pulled at me suddenly; Ping Ping's name had been called out. We went into consultation room number two. There was a divan for the patient to lie on, a table, several large posters illustrating the workings of traditional Chinese medicine and a small collection of rudimentary medical equipment. The lady doctor immediately inspired me with complete trust in her, however she would not look at me and talked only to Jessie. After the doctor had undressed Ping Ping herself, she felt his internal organs with her hands and looked at his tongue and his eyes for a long time. She did some tests on Ping Ping which I recognised: she laid the baby on his front hanging a small red ball on string infront of his eyes to get him to focus; she

51

scratched the undersides of his feet; she tried to get him to grip her fingers; she tried to make him sit up; she tried to make him support the weight of his head...

The frail grandmother with the crying girl came into the room, interrupted us, and pleaded with the doctor to see to her grandchild. The doctor sent her away. I remained standing and held Ping Ping while the doctor sat down at the desk and wrote four pages of detailed notes in the exercise book, stopping only to ask Jessie a few monosyllabic questions. The doctor then read out to Jessie what she had written. I cannot remember how I learnt that Ping Ping had Cerebral Palsy or that the doctor advised that he should remain in the hospital for immediate treatment; I do remember, though, how I broke down, helpless, sobbing on Jessie and holding her anorak for support. Without looking at me the doctor took Ping Ping from my arms to dress him. I noticed that the grandmother had come back in and was now sitting on a low stool in the room.

We returned to the main hall where Jessie called Mr Yu and the Director of the Registration office on her mobile. The Director told her to drive us straightaway to the Registration office with Ping Ping's little exercise book containing his medical report. I knew this meant that Chinese bureaucracy had taken over: Ping Ping would be sent back to Ping Jiang and our adoption of him would be officially cancelled.

*I held Ping Ping on my lap as I sat alone in a waiting room at the Registration office while Jessie handed over all Ping Ping's papers and his hospital exercise book to an official, possibly the Director, at the Registration office. This was awful. I knew that we could not care for Ping Ping; I also knew that the institution to which he was to be returned was not a good place for him. I asked Jessie whether we could pay for Ping Ping to remain at the hospital for treatment; I could tell from her expression that officialdom **had** taken over and Ping Ping had reverted to his previous status as a Ping Jiang orphan. He was helpless. I felt everything was hopeless. But as I carried him in my arms from the Registration office into the van for the long drive back to the hotel I promised him that I would not let him down.'*

'Poor O is in tears. I begin to dread that he will collapse with the grief, the disappointment, the cynicism, the ruthlessness, the betrayal of all the abandoned babies and the betrayal of us. Chung Chung listens to us and lets us talk on. She is being so good, so patient. She knows this is serious. And she listens, knowing that we will never keep the truth from her, that she is a very important part of it.'

We tried to reconcile the betrayal, if there was one. We looked at Ping Ping.

He was sinking deeper and deeper, moving further away from us.

We continued to wrestle with the whole thing, speculating and trying to adjust, struggling to reconcile a situation that was monstrous whichever way you looked at it, and therefore impossible to deal with fairly. It echoed the situation in China as a whole; how could any government deal humanely with the millions of abandoned babies in a country where the population currently runs at a fifth of the world's population? Humanity can't afford to be humane, it seems, when the population is so un-manageably huge.

'What is all this about, this endless, justifying talk about "twenty days"? Twenty days ago Ping Ping fell ill, says Mr Yu. They couldn't stop us coming, he says. Well, Mr Yu certainly could have contacted us by e-mail. That is, after all, how he asked us to contact him. Or did he assume that we wanted a boy at any cost? Did he think that serious illness is magicked away in the west because the west is rich? It seems extraordinary to me that this paralysing 'loss of face' actually requires and condones (by default) lying. It does seem that Mr Yu has, one way or another, lied to us and worse, that he has lied to us merely to avoid loss of face. To me any loss of face would come from lying, not the other way around. It seems that in China lying is collectively promoted almost as a noble characteristic and a natural, shared defence. Who then, defends Ping Ping in all this?'

We decided together that we would not try to replace him, and if we began the adoption process again it could only be when we knew that Ping Ping was properly cared for, when we all felt better about the whole thing, and when it was the right moment for Chung Chung.

We could not settle. The whole episode was shocking to us. For once in my life I would use the word 'nightmarish' knowing that it is the only meaningful description of how it felt. We could not understand what was behind the situation we were now in; were we in the hands of ignorance, greed, a desire to please, or wishful thinking? Or a ghastly mish-mash of all of these? How to explain this to a forbearing four-year-old who wondered why we were crying?

'A miserable room service lunch. Rice noodles and dry, western style salad with old, raw onion rings. We waited for Mr Yu until about four o'clock, but Chung Chung was desperate to get out...

O has taken her out for a walk. I have filmed my last minutes alone with Ping Ping who is still asleep, looking very smart and pathetically small in new

53

clothes for his return to Ping Jiang. I've packed all his stuff. This is agonising.'

When O and Chung Chung returned we took photographs of Chung Chung with Ping Ping. We said our good-byes in a cloud of grief. Jessie arrived very soon after with the 'vice-President' of Ping Jiang, a particularly short man, a peasant in a cheap nineteen forties style suit, very hard and very shiny shoes and an unfamiliarity with babies. Mr Yu, he said, was too busy to collect Ping Ping himself. Mr Yu, we all thought privately, was not willing to come himself to collect the baby. Nor had he seen fit to send a carer for the long journey. He had passed on his apologies, nevertheless, through his vice-President who handed O an envelope containing our 'donation', plus a small sum for compensation and a short note from Mr Yu hand-written in Chinese characters. It said;

"Dear Annabel and Olivier Stockman,

At the moment it is hard for me to find the right words to express my apologies. We should take the greatest responsibility for your failure to adopt. As we explained to you we only found out the kid's problem twenty days ago and have not had enough time to do further examinations, and also we didn't know he suffered from such a disease.

Sorry! Sorry!

We regret your family's wasted efforts and loss of money.

I was unable to come today because of a very important meeting I had to attend. Our vice-President Chen comes to you on my behalf with this letter expressing my sincerest apologies. And also with RMB 1,000 as compensation for your loss.

Yu 03.20.0"

No mention of Ping Ping's loss, or acknowledgement of his serious diagnosis by the doctor at the Hospital for Sick Children in Changsha, nor of any medical support Mr Yu proposes for him. Nor any mention of Chung Chung and her loss, nor her private, unexpressed sorrow...

Jessie was worried that Ping Ping was not warm enough. I unpacked his bag and pulled out his grubby yellow caterpillar trousers and jacket. Jessie nodded enthusiastically at the sight of quiltedness. She was so anxious for him to be warm that she put the clothes on him herself. Those yellow things seemed to be from so long ago; in fact we had been with Ping Ping from Sunday to Tuesday but it felt like years.

I had packed Ping Ping's original grimy layers, and almost all of the clothes we had brought with us for him, plus his nappies, bottles, baby milk, baby rice and his little toys. All the paraphernalia apart from a T-shirt and trousers Chung Chung had worn when we collected her.

The rough vice-President handed back our donation for Ping Jiang as "acknowledgement" for Ping Ping plus an extra hundred pounds in RNB for our "hurt and disappointment" - this in translation from Jessie. We did not yet know the contents of the letter from Mr Yu. Was the extra money a bribe? An apology? I wrote my feelings in our diary later. **'Only money really matters in China. And food. And face. Children are an expendable, common currency. The individual is no-man, no-name.'**

Jessie now had possession of Ping Ping, who was again hidden in a mass of yellow nylon quilting. The peasant picked up the bag, containing nearly everything we had brought for him. Zed Zed, a small stripey zebra fell out un-noticed onto the floor behind the peasant. I left it... Ping Ping is never likely to play with it as long as he remains in Ping Jiang... and we can keep Zed Zed as a keepsake, I thought.

After much loud talk between the vice-President and Jessie, a sudden movement away from our room. As we walked along the hotel corridor to the lift the peasant took possession of Ping Ping awkwardly and struggled to carry him and the carrier bag at the same time. His lack of experience with children was unsettling, even to Jessie. The pretty room service girls passed us pushing their trolleys stacked with crisp clean sheets, soaps, combs and toothbrushes in little boxes advertising the Hunan Furama Hotel. On Sunday we were smiling; today we must have looked grief-stricken. We waved goodbye helplessly to Ping Ping as he was carried into the lift. A surge of anguish rose in my chest and solar plexus as the lift door closed; my whole body felt about to shatter into pieces.

We stood at the window and watched the peasant in the car park waiting for his return ride to Ping Jiang. He walked up and down bouncing the yellow chrysalis roughly in his arms. I thought of the dreadful car journey ahead and this time not even a carer with him. How little they understood; they must have thought we didn't want him.

O and I flopped. Chung Chung asked why are you both crying? We tried to explain within her range of understanding, and a little bit more. No secrets. We all agreed that Chung Chung still did have a brother, though for the time being he would remain in Ping Jiang. If we were ever to adopt again, we would feel as though we had three children. Yes, Chung Chung replied, we would.

I had faxed Christine Manning at the Department of Health in London on Monday, in case we needed support. She had e-mailed the British Embassy in Beijing. Bernie Connolly now called us from the Embassy. She couldn't actually give us much direct help she explained to O, but this sort of thing was becoming more and more common, and she was there, and anything she could do...It wasn't much, but it was reassuring to know that they knew. China now seemed an awfully big place, and we felt alone in a sea of confusion.

'Ping Ping couldn't smile, except when something occasionally touched him in some way... a rare thing, sweet and dull at the same time. His was a thin, frail presence, silent, un-complaining, and inexpressive. Round eyes and weak bleats at a noise or the sensation of hot, cold or wet. Unresponsive to our sound and our touch.

Most pitiful of all was that he had tried to suckle. His hands searched my face as though he was blind. He buried himself in the dark crook of my shoulder. He whimpered and did not smile. I remember the whimpering now and my knees feel about to give way - something breaks again in my solar plexus - I don't want to hear that sound, that unbearably pathetic sound, so clearly as I do. We have become terribly fond of this little boy, this lifeless, impassive baby, at first even convincing ourselves that in our care he was enlivening.

How can Mr Yu and Zhong Ping say to us that he smiles often and eats meat and vegetables? He was delivered to us dirty and with a fungal infection behind the ears caused by his dribble as he lay on his back, presumably for hours, with no stimulation, care or interaction with other children. He smelled sour too, a smell that, in our brief time with him, did not leave him.

Chung Chung has done her best to play with Ping Ping. Changing his nappies, trying to carry him. She knew something was very wrong. She wanted to keep him. So did we.'

Later that afternoon drained and reeling, we tried to continue as usual; we walked to the shopping halls across the road from the hotel. The wide, pot-holed road was jammed with four lanes of me-first cars, buses, bicycles and pedestrians. Again, crowds of people registered surpise, shock even, at our being with Chung Chung, but they did not allow it to surface overtly. Even so, while some did scrupulously well at active lack of interest, others were drawn to us in a ponderous haze of semi-sleep, although there were no apparent reactions in their stares.

We wandered into a large space occupied by brand new white vans of all shapes and sizes. The next, clocks of all shapes and sizes. I saw another branded mark on a man's cheek. He was thin, and the mark was luminous, and thick magenta brushstrokes covered half his face. I was very shaken, affected by this sight. I now felt we were branded too. His back bent, the man shuffled slowly behind his wife as she shopped; the brand was his past, not hers... We moved through nondescript shoes into household goods. I hoped we might find a little something - an enamel bowl or plate decorated with animals or flowers, but this place was cheerless; it traded in their depressing reality, and unmitigated, hard, grey expediency: utility in an unsympathetic form. The place bore no resemblance to the Friendship Store we visited three years ago with Chung Chung. Then we had come away delighted with the resplendent plastic musical instruments and an enormous suitcase packed with dark "French" cloth which cannot be bought here.

But now in the halls I found the new Chinese enterprise culture depressing. The salesgirls looked under-fed, pathetic and aimless; they watched and studied us, blandly, at every step. Chung Chung fell asleep in O's arms. All the emotion and the strain of the place itself was too much for her - and us.

We heard a loud crack in the near distance, and a collective dull cry, then some angry shouts. We turned in the direction of a wide concrete staircase which announced the formal entrance to the halls. A large group of men in grey had collected like iron filings to a magnet. It *was* a magnet I suppose, for them. They were quick to join in. The group was holding a man back from another who was staggering from the blow we had heard. Everyone in the halls stood still, momentarily stunned in anxious suspense. Then the sickening smack of fist on cheek and head on concrete (a horrible sound in real life) echoed through the halls, and the uniformly grey men poured, as one, down the steps to follow the fighters who were intent on smashing the daylights out of each other on the hard steps.

China, this time, really felt very difficult for us. We hurried out, having bought nothing. We felt even more haunted by the confusion, the cruelty, the grisly drudge of day to day suffering for these desperately ignorant people.

'Room service in the evening, yet again. Phone calls; the misery of letting everyone know what has happened. Cancel the celebrations, move the cot out, somewhere, we don't care, just make disappear all the preparations for Ping Ping we wanted to say, but couldn't. O has called Christine. I called my mother. She is in tears, desperate for us to come home. O has changed our tickets to return to Beijing early, spending our time there instead of here while we wait until Sunday for the first flight home to London. We leave Changsha for Beijing tomorrow.'

O had a bath while Chung Chung slept soundly, weary and oppressed by the talk, worn to oblivion. Jessie called on the telephone to pass on Mr Yu's apologies (he had called her). I lay on my wide single bed, in semi-darkness, trying to rationalise it all. In between sips of Jamieson's I wrote my diary. What amazing foresight possessed O to suggest our diary, and for me to jump at the St Patrick's day priced bottles of Irish whisky? These must have been prompted by fate. Fate must have known we would have needed both. Fate must also have known that our adoption of Ping Ping would have gone wrong, in the most invisibly awful and self-inflicted way.

In between sips of whisky, brooding in the dark, I followed the steady breaths of Chung Chung's deep sleep, by turns comforted and intimidated by her trust in us. I could hear O in the bathroom sliding up and down the bath, reaching for soap with a whoosh! of water. The telephone rang again.

'A woman's voice, Chinese, announces to me in broken English that she is calling from "Ping Jiang Welfare" on Mr Yu's behalf. He comes on the line suddenly. I say "Hello, Mr Yu. How are you?" as though he must be suffering. He says something incomprehensible and stumbles...The woman takes over: "Yu Yong Gao apologise for hurt to you. He concern you not like him now". Impulsively I reply that "He shouldn't worry, we still have great respect for him!" I wonder whether I do now. I wonder whether his concern is the £600.00 we had been donating every year to Ping Jiang for care and medical expenses, none of which had been spent on Ping Ping. Anyhow we can't send him any money at the moment, we have no money to send. The woman presses on, now about how Mr Yu only knew of a serious problem twenty days ago. I tried to explain simply, through the fog of my drained state and the whisky, that the CCAA give foreign adopters every opportunity (should they wish) to reject a sick child in order to avoid this sad, confusing situation. The whole thing; the involvement of all these people, of the law, of Ping Ping and, of course, Chung Chung, did not have to take place solely because we had prepared for it; it could have been cancelled through the CCAA. What is more, our agency the Department of Health had approved us to adopt a healthy child, not a child with special needs. The woman ignored all this with an "Ah Mr Yu concern you not like him now". My head was reeling at this point with a combination of tiredness, confusion and irritation. I replied that we were very upset, exhausted, and that we had become terribly fond of the baby. "Ah! You fond of baby", she exclaimed. "When you get operation done?" I explained to the surprised woman that the Ping Jiang vice-President had returned with the baby to the orphanage this afternoon; we were fond of the baby, but we still had to send him back because of his serious health problems. "Ah! When you forget baby? Soon? You forget this baby from Ping Jiang soon? Ping Jiang have more baby for you!". She added, "You want new baby boy now? We have other baby boy!" "No!" I said, almost shouting. I thought about Chung Chung. Have they thought about how she feels? How will she look on this when she is older, realising that Ping Jiang did not look after Ping Ping in the way they looked after her?'

O fell asleep, beaten by his day which began early at the Hospital for Sick Children. The consultation had cost fifty pence. Pingjiang could have taken 3,600 children once each to the children's hospital in Changsha on the money Chung Chung had donated over the previous three years. Or 1800 children twice. Or 1200 children three times. Or 900 children four times. What had they spent the money on instead we wondered?

Chung Chung woke up later that night rather more energised and threw herself about, jumping on the beds. It seemed quiet and empty without Ping Ping. No whimpers or squeaks. No thin presence. No being with such lack of force, with such frail being-ness in our lives any more. We had become used to him in just forty-eight hours.

O woke up from a troubled sleep. At one a.m. he called his stepmother Maryvonne in Paris. When he heard her voice he wept into the phone in the dark unable to speak.

At 3.20 a.m. the telephone rang. We both awoke, almost delirious: an urgent fax must have arrived for us. Sustenance in the form of contact with those we trust. O eagerly agreed to open the door to collect the news. Instead a chambermaid passed him a fresh thermos of hot water...

Wednesday 21st March 2001, Aeroplane, Changsha - Beijing

At the end of a long, hair-raisingly fast car ride along the airport road which follows the swathes of red earth peculiar to Hunan, we skidded to a defiant stop at a changed Changsha airport. Like all the new buildings we saw in China the brand new high-tech version dominated the original, smaller and more modest airport. With plenty of new-build space available for extravagant monuments to money and business, earlier versions are not demolished to make way for their boorish offspring, they are merely ignored and left to decompose in their own time. So the brick airport we remembered surrounded by countryside now stood next to a great shiny silver hangar, every surface brushed aluminium, and marble flooring which was so slippery it seemed to self-polish. Signs of unemployment in the air, I wondered, and thought of China's strong desire to gain admittance to the World Trade Organization and to host the Olympics in 2008...All our young guides explained the dismissing of the old and venerable to make way for the new and shallow as a positive move in China, the new China, the China that is celebrating fifty years of Communism, but now as a new player in the world of Capitalism. Capitalism, I could see is now a 'good thing' in China. I thought of the Genoa Protests and the G8 Summits. I didn't pursue the issue...we were in China to collect Ping Ping, not to discuss the anomalies and differences between east and west economics. Besides there was a strong feeling of a party line in the young people allotted to us as guides. I didn't want to compromise their line, however fixed or fragile. The authorities, I thought, were already very trusting of us allowing us free access to the country and to their children. I didn't want to exploit that kind of trust. Anyway, insurmountable obstacles in communication appeared at every thought; I didn't have the energy, or the spirit, to take the subject on.

This time the queue at the check-in desk was affluent, celebrity status even, as we stood behind the eight-foot high Chinese star (stunt man?) we had first seen at Changsha railway station. He was still dressed from neck to ankle in the white racing-drivers' suit. Partly due (I speculated long and hard) to his lack of pockets, he had with him a short fat bodyguard in the regulation grey and pond-green who was carrying his passport, tickets and hand-luggage. Extraordinary to see them again, I thought, but then (despite our shambolic appearance) as westerners we belonged to the new "moneyed" class.

Jessie hovered close to us, keen to go, and keen, probably, to bring her responsibility of us to a close. It had not been the easiest of adoptions for her... and she must have questioned, even slightly, her own part in the

60

obfuscation of the facts. Maybe not. She had a small, grinding life to go to. There she would not have to torment herself with self-questioning; life was hard enough. She carried some of our bags to speed up our departure; she would have pushed to the front of the high-class queue if she had found a justification, however weak.

Behind us in the queue, to my astonishment was a Shaolin warrior monk. He manifested a modesty which was very pleasing in my stereotypical vision. I was curious to see that he was as well turned-out as any high-earning Chinese celebrity or politician. His saffron silk trousers were immaculately, sharply pressed and he wore an equally perfectly ironed silk robe draped with a simple white silk scarf. He carried a black leather bag which looked expensive, even by western standards. In it he carried his mobile phone and another, smaller, but equally expensive-looking leather pouch. I observed with admiration that his perfectly shaved head showed no history of any bumps or wounds. That is an achievement, I reflected, awestruck; it was evidence of his noble being and his skill as a Shaolin.

We were so anxious to leave Changsha that I had packed everything the night before with uncharacteristic speed and abandon. I felt we had to take the sentimental picture Mr Yu presented us with, but I gave the dolls to one of the pretty girls who made up the room, and I left the potty which Chung Chung despised so much - knowing that the chamber maids would giggle at it.

I visualised - with dread and yearning in equal measure - our imminent arrival home and I saw home so clearly in my vision that I saw no need to keep anything I had brought with us. While O and Chung Chung finally slept I walked around the room in the dark eliminating the last remnants of our 'failure' (as Mr Yu had so bluntly described in his letter) and anything else which brought back the reproach and the torment. I kept Zed Zed; after all, he was an innocent party in all of this.

We were anxious, too, to leave traces of the adoption behind. We were depressed about Ping Ping's condition and sickened by his lack of care. We were crushed by our failure to return home with him to an excited reception party and we dreaded a future without him, even though we had honestly accepted our mutual incompatibility. Feelings and questions thrown up by all this bewildered us. It felt like drowning by despair.

'The baby business thrives well in the new registration complex in Changsha city: the mothers give birth in the countryside and the babies make money for the province via hotels and offices in the city and the towns. No improvisation here, it seems, in Changsha; the system bears up very well to demand. Jessie

61

told us that Number One Orphanage in Changsha receives only one pound sterling per month from the State for the care of each baby...But for each baby adopted by foreigners the orphanage receives £3,000. On average five babies are adopted each week at Changsha Number One...all year round...'

Wednesday 21st March 2001, Later; Beijing City Hotel, Beijing

On the plane I wrote briefly in the diary, '**...extraordinary to think that the plane, taking one and a half hours, is covering the same ground that we travelled by train only four days ago. That journey seems months ago... Chung Chung seemed very little then...we were very different then...**'

I tried to immerse myself in Chung Chung's sticker book of dinosaurs because I found everything about the plane frightening. Whenever one of the men (I was the only woman passenger) squeezed out of his seat past the other sardines wedged together I could feel the plane tilt. Everything scared me, so I looked distractedly at the drawings in the book. I looked at pictures of dinosaurs and read descriptions of them intensely for the entire flight. Beside me O and Chung Chung were experimenting with the vacuum-sealed dried spicy plums which had been handed out by the flight attendants. On my other side a thin man was pressing acupressure points on his hands and wrist and spitting with a confident aim onto the small area of royal blue carpet between our feet. The girls wore lashings of slippery pillar box red lipstick and Country & Western meets the Stepford Wives aprons over their uniforms. Their eyebrows were drawn perfectly in smooth, unhesitating arcs.

As we trundled fast along a moving belt at Beijing airport O said he would ask Lida to ask Madame Fu to arrange a meeting for us with the CCAA. We would describe our situation and ask them if they would be prepared to keep our application "live" or open for, say, six months. This would give us time to organize placing Ping Ping in a hospital or a new family and to recover our senses before returning for another adoption. We would describe to them what had happened with Ping Ping; the confusion, the lack of communication, the inadequate translation by the guide. A general de-briefing which would help us and help them. The plan was comforting.

The new Beijing Airport was confident and gleaming, purring with efficiency and space. Our confusion, and then the silent chaos of filling out landing cards ended suddenly when we seemed to fall into the arms of Lida who was waiting for us at Arrivals. Our arrival did not have that sense of breathless euphoria that one sees in people so often. We were breathless when we told Lida everything; breathless from the tension, the lack of sleep, the fear of crumbling at the sight of what felt for us to be home and civilisation in the form of Lida. O asked her to call Madame Fu right away on her mobile telephone to arrange a meeting with the CCAA.

Jessie had called Lida to tell her we were returning early. What Lida did not know was how badly we felt, how raw we were: "Why you not forget baby and get new one?" she asked in the people-carrier as we rumbled along the highway, repeating our first drive to Beijing. I watched O as he sat facing Lida into the aisle gesticulating while the van bumped us in chorus over the holes in the road. He explained - successfully - that in the west this attitude is appropriate for a car, but not for a baby. Lida eventually seemed to understand the notion (one that rides against the general grain in China) and she pursued our cause with an impressive intensity of conscience. I do not believe that she ever truly understood our feelings, rather that she understood we felt that way, the western way, and that it was her responsibility to represent us.

We were full of our story - not angry or bitter - but bewildered, stunned, and very fearful for Ping Ping. We were going round in circles and being led to a sheer drop, an impasse ending in nothing. I could not make rational what I could not understand.

We waited for some time downstairs in the Beijing City Hotel for a 'family apartment' on a low floor. Had I accepted the apartment offered to us on the forty-second floor we would have been in it by now bouncing on the beds and trying out the TV. But the amount of time we were spending in lifts was demoralising me and the fear of being high up in tall buildings was showing itself under the general strain. We were in Beijing, most importantly, as a base for seeing the acrobats; still in the clouds of grief and defeat we were determined for Chung Chung to see her beloved acrobats and, so she hoped, the current incarnation of Li Li Ping, Champion Foot Juggler of 1965.

We were ushered into an apartment at the same moment as two young Mongolian women in old Nike trainers were unplugging large industrial vacuum cleaners from the walls. The place, of course, smelled strongly of tobacco and was enveloped in a queasy green illumination which seemed to transpire from the darkly tinted windows, and which at the same time suggested that there was piercing sunlight outside. There was a claustrophobic sense of airlessness in there, despite its extravagant size. The size worked strangely against it; it had a feeling of being 'unlet'; tired, sweaty nylon carpeting dotted generously with cigarette burns - fires even - especially around the sofa nearest to the giant TV, and large, lonely looking bathrooms which had seen years of coats of paint holding the plumbing together...I loved it. No pretensions, basic, and definitely self-catering. I looked into the two large bedrooms, the kitchen, the sitting room. Sparse and big. Just what we needed, I felt. The space was good. And a big TV set to disappear into to rest our systems which were on emotional overdrive.

Lida played with Chung Chung, admiring her and taking pictures of her doing her gymnastics. We were waiting to hear back from Madame Fu at BLAS to find out if we could have a meeting at the CCAA. I looked around the apartment and started to unpack a bit. I was struck by the heat. I looked out of a bedroom window onto the little, narrow streets below. The view was tantalising; festive swags of lights bobbed along the old, low buildings. From the hotel the small, cramped buildings seemed to pulse and hum with life. It looked cheerful. I longed to go down there and see for myself.

The call came at last: we were invited to come at ten a.m. tomorrow morning to see the Director, Guo Sijin. Lida raced off to her waiting people carrier and driver, reminding us to be in the foyer at nine-thirty a.m.

We were hungry: we hadn't eaten anything since breakfast. The vacuum-sealed dried fruits on the plane may have intrigued O and Chung Chung but had not fed them. We took the lift down one stop and arrived at the service floor; the business centre where one can fax and be faxed, restaurants, a beauty salon, and a tourist shop. Following the signs describing a four course fish menu we found ourselves facing yet another bank of small fish tanks, this one stacked from floor to ceiling and containing very unhappy creatures. Dark red curtains obscured the tall windows. The place was in semi darkness and the staff were mechanically laying tables and vacuuming solemnly; they were closed. Again, our synchronicity had slipped some cogs: it was four o'clock in the afternoon. We stepped down a wide circular staircase ending at the hotel foyer. The lobby was like a combination of the centerpiece of a shopping centre and the concourse of a train station. Swirls of pungent, sickly cigarette smoke unfurled steadily from the massed 'shiny-shoe-ed' occupants of a coffee bar which was raised on a dais for all to see and be seen.

The windowless breakfast room was empty but still open for brunch. As we waited to be served I followed the naively painted trellis and vine leaves positioned strategically around the bland white walls. Eventually, after the waitress had written down our simple order three times in longhand licking her pencil lead at the start of each character, we had chips and Heinz tomato sauce. This comfort food was accompanied by Chinese cover versions of Billy Joel songs booming from big speakers in each corner of the room. O asked the waitress - by pointing to the speakers and covering his ears - if the music could be turned down. At first she smiled, then she seemed to understand and then nodding enthusiastically went off purposefully. Nothing happened. It didn't matter. We had talked so much we had reached saturation. Besides we were ruminating on our morning

65

visit to the CCAA offices. We didn't have the spirit to speculate or plan out loud.

That night we tried to settle on the polyester sofa and concentrate on CNN as a treat, although the outside world and its doings seemed removed and inaccessible to me; it was as though my body couldn't take any more emotional pounding. The central heating was full on and we had unsuccessfully hunted for a switch to turn on the air conditioning instead. We were attracting static from the carpet, the furniture, the bedclothes, from virtually everything in the apartment. Every time any of us moved we crackled and sparked. The atmospherics felt taut, tense, and airless. I opened the windows a little to let in the city air. Beijing looked tall, and dark, the new buildings looming in the distance, ugly and coarse. Looking down I saw the little street decorated with lights and shop signs; a neon duck which alternated from pink to green was tempting. Another time, I thought, and we'd be down there amongst the restaurants, the hardware stores, the cake stalls, peeking into the alleyways stuffed to the rafters with trolleys, bicycles, chickens, washing, geraniums and babies. An agitated knock at the door, and one of the chambermaids rushed into the apartment waving and gesticulating at the windows. Knowing she could not tell us what she meant she closed the windows herself very firmly but with a gesture of apology, a gesture I felt covered our mutual lack of ability to communicate with each other.

We again played musical beds throughout the hot, airless night. I tried to remain completely still once I was in bed but the sheets seemed to generate static even when I thought about moving. I hallucinated all night that I was in a bouncy castle made of gorse bushes.

I woke up in a different bed from the one I went to sleep in. I had pulled the nylon sheets off the bed and rolled myself up in a blanket.

In the morning I went to the window and leant on the wide sill to look at Beijing. A thick yellow smog-like haze hung in the air. I couldn't see the tall, ugly buildings across the city. I couldn't see the little street down below us. I felt grit in my fingers; in fact the whole windowsill was covered with a thick layer of yellowish brownish purplish sand; it was the dust from the loess storms which blow down into Beijing from the Mongolian steppes every Spring. At the window the yellow-violet dust hung in the air as though suspended in an airless void.

Thursday 22nd March 2001, Beijing City Hotel, Beijing

We had breakfast amongst the trellised vines, surrounded this time by quite a crowd. A very interesting crowd; Russian, Azerbaijani, Uzbeki. Men who looked like oil rig workers and their decorated, older-looking and overweight wives who dyed their hair jet black or peroxide blonde.

A tall fair-haired western man walked in carrying a young Chinese baby. The baby was bright, alert, upright, looking around with interest. A clarity of understanding appeared in me at that moment which caused me physical pain; I had been convinced by my desire, and blind to the reality which first faced us: the reality that Ping Ping wasn't right...for us. How could I have not seen it immediately? A lack in myself revealed itself then. Despite O's reservations I had clung to my vision that everything could be OK. I was deceiving myself. I had caused even more pain and confusion for all of us. That's how it was when I saw that healthy baby in the arms of the tall, blond westerner...

Over our bouncy cotton-wool toast and jam we spoke about the proposal we would make to the CCAA. We would not complain, at all - how can one complain about life? No, it would take probably (accounting for pleasantries and translation) about ten minutes for us to request a moratorium on our application. Then, having agreed on that, we planned a nice day out. The Buddhist Fayuansi Temple in the Muslim quarter, the Foreign Languages Bookstore, the acrobats in the evening. The champion Chinese acrobats had become a fascination for Chung Chung, a source of pride almost, when she could flirt with the notion of Chinese beauty, strength and skill, and of her being Chinese too. The lady acrobats in the films made by the Beijing Education and Scientific Film Studio had become role models and she would fall into her own routine of calisthenics cum south London gymnastics whenever she saw available floorspace, anywhere.

We visualised an early morning visit to the Temple of Heaven south of the Imperial Palace in the Chongwen district the following morning for Chung Chung to see the city elders practising Tai Chi. We would also ask Lida to take us to a small park somewhere, a place where people flew kites on Fridays...

Lida was tense, and late (we subsequently realised her lateness was normal). The driver was, as usual, smiling and prepared for anything. Driving across Beijing from the northeast section of the city to the southwest corner, it became apparent that Lida didn't understand about

67

kites and that anyway serious kite-flyers were using the canal towpaths which run beneath and beside the roads. As we drove along the big roads - the freeways - at speed, eagles, moths, butterflies and grasshoppers were flying above us, held from below on long lines.

Lida introduced us to her BLAS colleagues in their small office situated within the CCAA building. Madame Fu was sharp, quick and in charge. There were two other young guides and 'translators' like Lida making travel arrangements on the phone. One was preparing to take a group of Norwegians to Yunnan. The other was on the phone to a registration office clarifying the place, day, and time for a group of foreign adopters. Had it not been for our unconventional request, Lida would have been finalising arrangements for a large Spanish group to go to Fujian to adopt their babies. We sat in their offices, politely drinking green tea for some time. Nothing was said to us about the wait, but Chung Chung was flagging and she had caught a head cold on the plane. We ventured to ask about the delay; it was sunny outside and we were looking forward to our visit to the Fayuansi, the Temple of the Source of Buddhist Teaching.

The temple was a walk away from the CCAA building in the old Xuanwu district and I wanted very much to see it. The guidebook described it as the oldest temple in the inner city of Beijing, completed in 696 AD, and now the centre of Buddhist teaching, training young monks as young as four to enter monasteries in China. Apart from the need to turn my mind to something other than Ping Ping, I was genuinely excited by the chance of seeing this disregarded and venerable place.

In a moment Lida was leading us on thick, springy carpeting through the plush corridors of the CCAA offices and past expensively mounted blown-up photographs of smiling white Americans with their adopted babies. The highly polished heavy mahogany doors all carried shiny brass name plates and numbers. Christine Manning who works in poorly maintained, cramped offices at the Department of Health building in Waterloo would be awestruck at the comfort of these government offices.

We were led into a large, long room in which was installed the 'CCAA Exhibition': hundreds of mounted photographs of Chinese babies and children, all looking happy, some with tremendous handicaps and deformities who were all smiling hard. It was a shocking exhibition; clearly the CCAA were proud of their work, and proud of the children but it was the quantity of these pictures of Chinese children with westerners - mostly Americans - which took my breath away. I looked with amazed disbelief at the group photographs of westerners with their adopted Chinese babies who were suffering from very serious problems. I sank into the carpet,

68

riveted to a picture of a smiling little girl in the ubiquitous lace mob-cap in a wheelchair, surrounded by a large blond happy family, her stumps for legs just showing under her pink gingham dress. The Stars and Stripes flew from a pole in the garden behind them. Reproach appeared and screamed at me.

In the centre of the room there were three large trunks containing hundreds upon hundreds of thick files tied together roughly with string. We read the labels. Spanish names and addresses neatly typed, Canadian, Swedish, British, Irish, Dutch, American...these were the dossiers of applicants for adoption which had not yet begun the year long adoption process. If those people knew their files were stationary in this way, I thought, they would surely weep with frustration. Lida announced proudly in her tour guide tone that the CCAA had processed 7,000 applications last year.

Like the files, we had hung around here for far too long. Chung Chung had been temporarily occupied by the photographs, but she was tired and she needed air and food. We asked Lida when we were going to see the Director. Lida disappeared for a while and returned beaming. She announced that the CCAA Director and all the staff live in the same building and that they had all had to stay at home this morning for gas repairs, so she would show us their offices while we waited. The offices were bright and cheerful, spit-spot clean and very, very organised; ship-shape to process tons of files.There were large windows on one side of the partitioned offices which opened the place up to a big blue sky, trees, leaves fluttering in the breeze and a crowd of rough, smudged sparrows chirping loudly in the branches.

This was very pleasant but, a hiatus appeared; we ventured once more... "Perhaps after lunch..? Perhaps later sometime they will be back from waiting in for the gas man?" To profit from the time while she considered this, I went to the ladies' lavatory at the end of the Hall of Happy Foreign Adoptions. It was hotel-comfortable; dark terracotta-tiled, and clean, with hidden down-lighters spotlighting the way, automatic taps and hand-driers, and a deep, sour- smelling hole in the floor.

Lida insisted we drive to the Fuyansi Temple, though we had said that it was within walking distance and that in any case we wanted to walk. In blistering, white sunshine we drove round and round, and up and down the hutongs and alleyways of the ancient city of Beijing. Both Lida and the driver had never heard of our temple. They began to argue. They both jumped out of the taxi at unexpected moments to pounce on passers-by and demand to be told how to find it. There is no apparent preamble required by society in China for a request from a stranger; an innate sense of mutual equality seems to invalidate any need for an expression of courtesy, and, for that matter, of apology. The driver seemed to become desperate, as though his honour depended on finding the place. Honour seemed to be more important, and seemed to say more about status, than how one dealt with others. He squeezed us and his dented taxi down alleyways with an inch to spare either side while I gazed at the old buildings in horror.

'The hutongs have been smashed down as though there has been a war. What we saw reminds me of war photographs of houses in villages in Bosnia, Croatia, Palestine, after the destroyers have left. The broken, ancient walls of once important, rich courtyard villas surrounded by the rubble of bricks and dust. A large basket was swinging slowly in a breeze, balancing on the remaining corner of what had once been a grand doorstep flanked by lions, and what had been in the last fifty years a shared doorstep for many families, for an entire community. A sock hung from the remaining lintel of a door. The buildings and the homes are ravaged. It looks like the pictures I've seen of war.'

The temple was located with surprising understatement. The car came to a slow, rolling halt, the driver got out and spoke in familiar terms to a knife grinder he had only just slid past by a hair, and jumped back in again lighting a cigarette with a flourish of triumph and finality. He had done his job; he was, as it were, 'over and out' - for the duration, and he expected the duration to be a long one.

Lida accepted, with a distracted, disbelieving look that the temple was Buddhist, not Muslim. There were big, friendly stone lions sitting at the wide courtyard gates, with big, square grins and deep-carved curls tumbling about their heads. So smiley and welcoming in benign guardianship that they almost looked like dolphins.

Leathery-skinned beggars from Mongolia and Heilongjiang hung around outside the grand, faded red gates demanding money. Three thin, very rough men saw us and rushed at us with their hands out, intoning "Eloor! Gimme, gimme, gimme!" Pushy, persistent and insistent. I retorted, "We're not Americans!" I don't know why I said it. I knew perfectly well that the American adopters who came to China were ordinary people like us, with ordinary means. I think it was that the beggars assumed that we were American, and American commerce was creeping insidiously, and successfully into China; the MacDonald's in Qianmen Xi Dajii (the largest in the world and close to a Kentucky Fried Chicken) was used regularly by

70

all kinds of Beijingers. I thought of the court case in Britain of 'McLibel' in 1990, and Jose Beauvais v. McDonald's (and anything else to do with American commercial globalisation). With this kind of cultural impact from the US, it did not occur to the Chinese we met that Britain could be a different country. I was keen too that Lida should be made aware of a difference between the British and the Americans. My bad-tempered remark worked. I saw the notion land in her mouth; she chewed on it, looking perplexed but she seemed to awaken, even if momentarily, to something relatively subtle.

The courtyard was dry, dusty, faded, and the sun shone in soft patterns across it. Plane trees grew between old, uneven, and softly worn flagstones. This place was wonderful. It was good and warming. It was peaceful. We began to frolic almost in the exhilaration of calmness. The air was clean and sweet. The work of the place had a civilising effect on the air, it seemed; it was nourishment for me and I felt a surge of happiness. Shaven-headed monks in flowing saffron robes walked noiselessly across the courtyard. I anticipated the temple as though it was to be the meal of my life. Lida, unimpressed and clearly unimpressionable, studied the opening times and the cost for entrance to the temple.

I tried to absorb and understand the place; the layout and the architecture of the temple itself and its courtyard. I saw faded red, peeling walls where layers of plaster had fallen away over the centuries. I saw two imposing lions, with their smiles and curls still, now guarding three steps to the temple doors. The rest I could only feel; the air, the gentle sound of the courtyard, the stillness of the life of the place. It was as though my eyes were not big enough to see what I demanded them to see. Now my memory of the temple is fragmented, limited by my inability at the time to see unselectively like a camera, and coloured by my tension and my desire.

Chung Chung and I ran over to a small building, almost an out-house, fashioned like a temple and situated inside the courtyard walls. Scaffolding leant heavily against it on one side and against another, a nineteen fifties dusty pea-green shelf unit. I lifted her up to look through the broken window in a small door on one side. Many identical hand-sized figures of a seated Buddha, one headless, were stacked one above the other in a dusty heap, and around them in their hundreds, covered also in a thick layer of dust, were parcels of books wrapped in brown paper, now faded, and tied with string. 'Curioser and Curioser' Alice said. So did we.

The Watchman was out for his lunch, Lida told us. We couldn't go in to the temple. We wouldn't be able to see the Buddhas inside today. Tomorrow...I thought, tomorrow we'll come back, tomorrow we'll have a picnic, tomorrow we'll see the temple and we will find out about the small dusty Buddhas and the dusty books. Now, though, we had to go back. We needed to have lunch before we met the Director, at one-thirty, Lida said.

The taxi driver was smoking and laughing, leaning across the bonnet of his car. He was in loud, animated conversation with one of the beggars. A moment of clarity appeared to me then; in my state of grief and exhaustion I saw China as a society of equality: not a society of feeling, nor of conscience, but of cruel disinterest, of cold-bloodied equality.

Chung Chung was ratty, querulous and became progressively more and more tired during lunch at the restaurant near the CCAA offices. Energy in the form of noodle soup and vegetables in oyster sauce did nothing for her. She uncharacteristically demanded to keep her set of white porcelain chopstick stands in the form of seated lions. Lida, ever conscientious about her responsibilities, bought them when she paid the bill. I was surprised; in Europe the 'patron' or the 'maitre d'Hotel' (in the interests of good relations and the indulgence of children) would have given them to Chung Chung, with a big show, of course. I thought about it, children are openly adored in public in China, in a fawning and near-hysterical way that one wouldn't expect from an otherwise apparently inexpressive people. I thought again, as we left the restaurant, nodding our heads in thanks, maybe it is quite simply - in this still feudal society - the sex of the child which governs the response, public or private.

Lida took us directly to the office of the CCAA's Deputy-Director-General, Zhang Zhong. A smiling-eyed man, he rose from behind his desk to greet us. He seemed to be wearing a dress suit for a wedding. He walked over to us, shook our hands, and warmly and politely gestured for us to sit down on the black leather slippery three-seater. He settled, still smiling, into a large black leather swivel chair, an original Eames chair it looked to me.

Behind the Deputy-Director's desk sprawling over the entire wall were dark shelves supporting quantities of books about Chinese adopted children. On another wall, by the water dispenser, hung a large nineteen twenties sun-faded oil-cloth map of China. Against our wall - the opposite end of the office from his desk - was the long black leather sofa and a painting above it, a painting I cannot remember at all because I sat beneath it, trembling, as we told our story through Lida. The fourth side of the office had a big window with a clear view of the sparrows fighting and chirruping in the top branches of the big plane trees outside. The light from that window I can remember clearly now; the intensity and clarity of the light couldn't have been like that in London. I made an appointment with myself to look at a world map to compare other cities on Beijing's line of latitude: Samarkand,

Ankara, Naples, Madrid, Baltimore, Indianapolis and Denver...

Zhang Zhong asked what he could do for us, still relaxed, talking slowly, moving slowly. There was something reassuring and gentle about him. I jumped in, trying to be measured, and began our story. Lida interpreted with more noise and vigour than I had intended to express and she took over the conversation like a barrister defending us in court, standing as she shouted, and gesturing violently in her pinstripe trouser suit. She told the Deputy-Director that we had been cheated. She pointed at us and told him how desperately upset we were, too upset to replace Ping Ping. He looked at me squarely, kindly, "You asked for a special needs baby". "No!" we replied, shocked by the bluntness of this notion, "Mr Yu suggested that we apply to you for Ping Ping. We understood only that he had a split lip." "Well, you know," he said, shaking his head slowly, and glancing meaningfully at the map, "you need to understand something about China: the countryside is very great in size and there are many, many orphanages and there are - we don't know how many - orphanage directors who are not always qualified to do the job". I stopped trembling and went cold instead. I was overwhelmed by the realisation that there was a rational explanation for Mr Yu's actions, and that this was in part due to our own lack of understanding of the Chinese. I understood now that a split lip in China means serious problems. Zhang Zhong had just described Ping Ping's split lip as "special needs". Mr Yu had written on the envelope, "Are you sure about this?"

In China the condition seems to be related to other, more serious physical problems. In the affluent, well-fed west a split lip generally is not significant...So, yet again, I lamented inwardly, a big misunderstanding, but this time a monumental one.

I was impressed by this man's simplicity and intelligence. It seemed to me that I had been mildly reprimanded. I now felt responsible for the misunderstanding with Mr Yu, and ashamed of our ignorance of real China and its ways. The arguing sparrows still scuffled noisily in brilliant leafy sunshine. I thought about Ping Ping now presumably lying on his back again in Ping Jiang, alone. I remembered those photographs of Ping Ping that Mr Yu had sent us. Photographs of him sitting upright in a high chair with his lip corrected, but not his palate. Photographs that must have been set up, the ubiquitous supporting hand hidden out of shot. Those kind of contrivances may not seem, at first, to have much to do with cultural differences but rather, to do with betrayal; it's possible, though, that Mr Yu was hoping that we could take the baby and - once in our arms - would take the baby, for the baby's sake. Feelings of failed responsibility and helplessness for Ping Ping welled up in me into a constriction. Barely able

73

to breathe, I was about to stand up, politely offering heartfelt thanks, my hand outstretched, and go.

The Deputy-Director looked at us again, kindly. "You should not go home without doing what you intended to do. Please stay. Find another baby. A healthy baby. We can arrange this for you immediately." Through Lida we tried to describe our feelings for Ping Ping, how, in a short time we had loved him, and how we felt terrible responsibility for his return to Pingjiang, but that our immediate responsibility was towards Chung Chung who, like us, was desperately disappointed and yes, still needed, and wanted, a brother. I added that there had been so many misunderstandings...I couldn't speak anymore; my throat had tightened, my eyes spilled tears with the promise of help out of this dark place. "We will find you your healthy baby", he said, " but first let me meet your little daughter."

Chung Chung had been downstairs with Sarah (her English name) in the BIAS office. She was sitting playing contentedly on the desk with a baby doll next to Sarah who was supposedly working out her travel plans on the computer but was actually playing with her. Chung Chung, not a doll girl, was fascinated by the doll's innards; each time she was squeezed she gurgled something in Chinese. This was an intriguing concept. We brought Chung Chung upstairs to meet Zhang Zhong. The ladies from the various 'Archive' departments who process the files and the post-adoption reports joined us. Chung Chung beamed at them all and demonstrated her Chinese acrobat inspired 'calisthenics' on the round carpet of blue and white clouds. They were delighted by her and applauded loudly. We had met the women the previous July in London when a CCAA delegation had paid an official visit to the Department of Health. They were more sophisticated and better educated than the young people we had met in the shops and hotels; except for the language, their painted eyebrows, and their large, colourful flasks of tea, in their manners these women could have been western.

After a short indulgence of Chung Chung, reciprocated smiles and handshakes of mutual recognition, Zhang Zhong asked Chung Chung if she would like a little brother or a little sister. Had she said 'sister' we would probably have been able to walk round the corner to Beijing Number One Welfare Institution to collect a nice little girl and retire, exhausted and grateful to our large, but static-prone apartment at the Beijing City Hotel.
Now quite drained of any healthy energy and running on adrenaline I tried to relax and smile as we all held our breaths waiting for her decision. Only a few moments before I had been preparing to walk away from all this. Now I was anticipating the notion of another baby, a new being I had never thought about until now. Zhang Zhong explained that there were a few boy

74

babies here in Beijing orphanages, though all of them had split lips and therefore unknown associated problems; it was our choice but he would recommend a known healthy baby. He looked steadily at us. "There is one available healthy baby boy in China," he said quietly, "but he is not here in Beijing."

Chung Chung was aware that everyone was waiting for her decision and that it was hers to take. How to face our precarious vacuum and leap wholeheartedly into the void making it alive again: these decisions now rested with Chung Chung and Zhang Zhong. O and I had run out of the stuff that decisions are made from; we were dizzy from thinking too much. I felt relief that fate was in control now. I pictured us now in the safety of Zhang Zhong's office and the events of the last days and weeks, and I was reminded that fate may have been in control all along.

Chung Chung announced that she wanted a little brother. At once I was enormously relieved and daunted by the prospect of more travelling. I tried to visualise a healthy baby boy who was not Ping Ping. In one moment I was bloated with grief and consumed by a new excitement. Zhang Zhong and the "Archive" ladies smiled big smiles and applauded her again. "*Didi!*" ("Little Brother!") they chorused. Chung Chung continued, "I want another little brother, because I have one already but he isn't well enough to come home with us".

We all moved off and downstairs into an Archive office directly beneath the Deputy-Director's office. Another black leather sofa, in the same position, but this time facing the neatly divided working areas, all with computers and neat filing systems. I remember noticing that nobody fought with the photocopier as we do in the office here. It all seemed terribly organised, smooth-running and harmonious. The sparrows on the lower branches outside in the sunshine and the large tea flasks decorated with red and orange chrysanthemums - stowed neatly - made the office feel positive, happy, lively ... productive.

The women began to prepare the file of the baby boy along with their official offer of him to us. They were smiling all the time. The speed of all this was extraordinary for us: in adoption applications to China, from the time our applications arrive in the CCAA offices to the moment their offer of a baby arrives with us can take anything from nine to fifteen months. I now realised that their processing for our Ping Ping application had also been fast: they had remembered us from our meeting with them in London, and in our application we had specified a named baby who, in their judgement, had special needs status.

Lida went back to the BLAS office to catch up on her preparations for her Spanish group. Exhausted from the excitement and relieved to witness a dramatic change in atmosphere Chung Chung curled up on the soft, black leather and fell into a state of near hibernation. We were offered large glasses of water and we sat, sipping them, watching the women in the office. I was now in a state of numb euphoria, almost insensible. Like Chung Chung I could have leaned sideways a few degrees and disappeared into stupor.

The youngest of the women spoke very good English. She did much of the translating at the CCAA. She showed us that they had received our most recent adoption follow-up report for Chung Chung. Smiling, she opened the file at the photographs of Chung Chung at home with us. The women laughed indulgently and joked while some used the photocopier and others were on the telephone. The eldest of the women, and most senior in the hierarchy, brought a smart brochure over to us to look at. It was an expensively put together resume of the CCAA's activities and successes in 2000. She pointed to one of the pages. There was a beaming Chung Chung, in social mode, in the arms of Guo Sijin during the CCAA's visit to London. There was no point waking her to see it, she was deeply asleep.

As Chung Chung slept we saw the first photographs taken of our new little boy when he was eight months old. An intense baby, with a soft black shock of hair and a darkly uncertain gaze sliding beyond the camera, and fierce eyebrows, in symmetrical, knotted arabesques. He was in a vest decorated with small baby-pink roses. This contradicted his determined posture, his small shoulders up by his ears. We were shown more pictures of him lying on his front on a bamboo mat outside on grass and sitting on a bamboo mat in a wide, square metal cot inside the orphanage. I looked at him, this strong character looking purposefully away. Struggling with the significance of it all I tried to focus and to imagine what this little being must be like now, at fourteen months.

The sudden 'offer' in the form of this tiny photograph of a serious baby boy with a comical look was stupefying. We looked and talked, looked and talked, and talked and talked....

The ladies hovered, smiling. Lida, now with us again briefly, translated the baby's medical report along with comments about him from the orphanage. He was naughty, they all repeated, delighted by the notion, and giggled. Lida mentioned that the ladies were still waiting to know whether we would accept the baby... or not. We did not need to discuss this. We signed our acceptance form immediately, unaware that we had been holding up the process...

Our 'permission to travel' to collect the baby was then put in front of us on the table to sign. We signed immediately. It was now all done. The CCAA had contacted the orphanage to check that the baby was still fit, they had spoken to the local registration office to book a time for the official adoption to take place with all parties present, they had spoken to the local Notary, and they had passed on the details to Lida and Madame Fu at BLAS for them to plan the travel itineraries and to book a guide to help us through the process there.

We remained - almost frozen by the speed of all this - at the table clutching the baby's photograph and his reports. We had no idea where he was 'residing' or what his name was. In the excitement the ladies had not thought to tell us.

Zhang Zhong came back into the office, still smiling of course, and now looking very pleased. It was clear that it was time to go back downstairs to the BLAS office. Chung Chung had to be woken up very gently; I didn't want the Deputy -Director and the ladies to see how cross she can be when she wakes up from a deep sleep.

As we shook hands and smiled and expressed our thanks for their work that afternoon, O asked them the baby's name. "Hua Jijun!", they all said, "Magnificent Military Discipline!". "What name are you going to call him?" asked Zhang Zhong. Well, we said, we had chosen the name "Chung Chung" because of the sound and because it means China (Zhong Zhong). He said, "In that case call her baby brother "Hua Hua", which means Magnificent, and then you have "Chung Hua" (correctly, Zhonghua): "Magnificent China". I asked where we would be going to collect the baby. Zhang Zhong pointed to a bright, modern map on the wall above the sofa. He pointed roughly southeast, near the sea; there was no translation and we lost where the baby was living into the general frantic void. I pictured the challenge of more aeroplane excursions and tried very hard not to sit back down again. As the Deputy- Director shook hands with us for the last time he gave us his card. He smiled. "If you have any problems adopting your new baby, let me know."

Downstairs Lida and Madame Fu showered us with BLAS presents; wallhangings, red paper cut-outs, Peking opera masks on red tassels, little figures in ethnic costume, and an overtly westernised mother and baby drawing in a picture frame with 'Blas' in little gold letters along the side. To keep Chung Chung happy they offered her bright boiled sweets, calling them "candies". This Americanism startled her. To occupy us they showed us many group photographs of their Spanish, Canadian, American, Dutch and Danish adopters, all standing in a line for the camera clasping their babies and grinning with tired excitement. Chung Chung could not remain politely awake any longer and burrowed back into their black leather sofa.

While we sipped green tea and looked politely at the photographs, Lida and Madame Fu began working on the travel arrangements. Lida hurriedly scribbled a list of fees for travel and hotels and Madame Fu, who was seated at a desk obscured by a mound of papers, pens and clips in front of a gigantic map of China, shouted into two telephones at once, one instrument at each ear. Like the Archive women upstairs, Madame Fu smiled as she worked, loud and fast.

Lida and O sorted out the refund on our cancelled flight back from Changsha, and this went towards our new, unexpected, travel expenses. I looked at the map of China from a distance; Madame Fu was pointing in the direction of Shanghai. Definitely another tense plane ride, I thought, but I still wanted to travel again by train. A pretty lake town was mentioned where the adoption would take place. It was half an hours' flight from Shanghai... or an hour and a half away by train. It was agreed that we would fly to the lake town near Shanghai to collect and adopt Hua Hua, we would then travel by train to Shanghai to get him a travel visa from the British Consulate. From Shanghai we would catch the plane home to London. The train, we said, was cheaper and more beautiful and more peaceful and it would be Hua Hua's first train ride and the train ride would be ideal for our early days with Hua Hua. Lida had her disbelieving look again, giggling that the Chinese moneyed, upper classes always travel by plane, and so did she. Madame Fu smiled at our sense of romance and shouted into the phone to order tickets for the train.

'More and more dazed, we are still being carried in the eye of the storm - now positive. Beijing and China begin to gleam and shine, the dust blown away by our change in fortune. In the people carrier on our way back to the Beijing City Hotel, I looked at China differently; I wanted to return, I wanted to be here again on different terms: I wanted time to know it more, knowing that I wanted to love it more, hoping that I might one day understand it more. '

In London we had promised Chung Chung an outing to the Acrobats. It had to be this evening after our long day at the CCAA since this was our last night in Beijing. Our late outing felt delightful; so easy and so simple compared with our recent adventures. We were driven through the drizzle gazing at the crowds of people filling the streets and at the flickering lights of glittery night-time Beijing. We had a renewed sense of adventure now, and a satisfaction that despite all our difficulties we had managed to pull off the biggest treat for our stoical Chung Chung, who was still passionate about Chinese acrobatics.

Late into the night while O and Chung Chung slept in high voltage sheets, I shuffled our things around for final packing for the plane to Hangzhou - the seventh time I had wrestled with stowing or finding in the last eight days. I thought about Ping Ping, Mr Yu, his wife, Zhong Ping, Stella, Jessie, the Director of the Registration office in Changsha, the lady doctor at the hospital for sick children, the vice President of Ping Jiang, Lida, Zhang Zhong, the Archive ladies, Madame Fu, the Buddhist monks, our drivers, the chambermaids.... and the resident drunk at the theatre this evening who had lurched around smiling coyly at us from the orchestra pit while we sat in the front row dazzled by the preposterous feats of poise and balance of the acrobats...

'I look at the looming buildings in the distance scattered with jewelled squares of light, and while I pack, change my mind and re-pack, receiving shocks all the while, Ping Ping is on my mind. I want to return to the Fuyansi Temple and learn about the dusty Buddhas. But I'm too tired to use my mind sensibly at all.'

Friday 23rd March Aeroplane Beijing - Wanghu Hotel, Hangzhou

Lida and the smart van picked us up early for Beijing Airport. Dry, tired, headache-y, we were almost staggering at each step. Lida, on the contrary, was bright and cheerful, exhilarated by her success. As a gesture of friendship Lida gave Chung Chung a CD of children's songs. They sat next to each other in the van, singing.

Like all new public buildings in China, Beijing airport has been designed with the traveller's comfort in mind and the lavatories are the best I have come across. However, I remember with nostalgia our first arrival at the old airport in 1998 when we came to adopt Chung Chung. Our guide Doris was not at the arrivals gate to meet us. O had gone to find a phone box in the hope of speaking to Madame Gao -the equivalent of Madame Fu- in French (she had lived in Paris for some years) to find out what we should do. I waited for him in the entrance hall, watching the workmen in their blue overalls repairing lights and door hinges and the young women in pink overalls polishing the floor and picking up cigarette ends in their small, delicate fingers. Petals of plum blossom swirled in on a gentle breeze through the open glass doors into the hall; an irony: they were beautiful, poetic, but the girls chased them and picked them up by hand. A Haiku poem in motion, I thought.

I wept when we said goodbye to Lida. She hugged Chung Chung at floor level - the Chinese always squat at the child's level - and she gave us letters to read, with instructions to open them when we had gone through customs. We sat in unimaginably comfortable seats looking out at our waiting aeroplane. The letter to Chung Chung read at the top "I Love You" with, underneath, the Chinese equivalent.

"Dear Chung Chung,

You are so luckly to have such great parents. They love you so much. I deeply appreciate the way of your parent educate. I learn too much from them and get some idea for how to rise my own child in the future.

My dearest Chung Chung, It's hard for Lida to forget a such pretty, bright and promising girl. I don't think that I can forget the wonderful time we spent on. I hope of course you can. You have a peaceful and happy life. May your Dad, Mum, you and Hua Hua are health, happy, and enjoy your life very well. Lida pray for your kind family in the another side of the world.

I hope I can kiss you again.

I know your birthdy is coming around, so I give you a CD for famous Chinese Children's song as a gift of birthday. Hoping you like it.

Happy Brithday to you!
Lida"

And to us Lida wrote;
"Dear Annabel and Oliver,

I think you are luckly too for having a such extremly bueaty, and clever daughter with your life. She likes a Angel.

I terribly understanding your feeling about this unhappy matter. But from another aspect to think about it again, I think you are luckly.

You learn much from that, but also have a unforgetable exprensue in your life. I think everthing arrange by God and Hua Hua maybe originally belong to you. You needn't feel too upset, but just think God make a kidding with you. Because God wants to give you and us (Blas, CCAA) some lessons. Both of us can learn much from that. What do you think? please cheer up! You will have more happy with Hua Hua, so whyn't happy, I think no matter Ping Ping or Hua Hua, they are no diffrent. OK?!

Looking forward to hearm from/ seeing you.
May you have a plesent trip in China!
Sincerely yours, Lida"

Tears appeared again at the notion that God had played tricks on us and Ping Ping, and that Lida had felt obliged to encourage us to stop caring. No, O said, we don't stop caring; we will find Ping Ping new parents.

Chung Chung sang and talked throughout the two-hour flight. I wrote our diary with a renewed hope. O studied the 'Rough Guide to China'. He found that old Hangzhou is a beautiful place which "attracts Chinese holidaymakers all year round and especially in the summer because it benefits from the gentle sea air rolling in from the east China Sea. The countryside is fertile and on one side the town surrounds West Lake, large and peaceful and dotted with islands and promontories with museums and temples for meditation." The "Temple of Autumn Moon on Calm Lake", the Botanical Gardens and the stone Buddhas at Feilai Park inspired me. O read out some basic information, the first, that new Hangzhou is not a town as we were told, but more like a city by our standards. The Chinese, it said, describe Hangzhou as "The Paradise on Earth". I was impressed by that description contrasting with our last impressions of grey Changsha and embarrassed by our ignorance about Hangzhou, given that we had had two years to prepare our second visit to China.

We were booked in at the Registration office that afternoon for the official adoption. We had first learnt about Hua Hua yesterday and today we were due to become his legal parents. I reminded O that Hua Hua needed a

81

name, a name we all agreed on, and that we needed to decide now and not at the registration office. We had given Ping Ping the names Jack Ping Ping Louis Jiang Xiao Hu Stockman. I had always been in love with the name Louis, and O's hero is Buster Keaton and so it came to be that Hua Hua's names were to be Louis Hua Hua Buster Jijun Stockman. We did not know how to spell Hua Hua's first name, "Military Discipline" ("Jijun" in Pinyin Chinese), or how big he was, or where his orphanage was or where we were going. We were again carried by events, knowing that this time they were taking us in a happier direction. I felt a gradual, slow shift of feeling; this dark, small place I had been in was opening towards light. I wrote on the plane:

'We have the right names for our new baby. Our other baby is to have new parents, the right parents. How this happens I cannot imagine, but I believe absolutely that O can make it happen. Through us Ping Ping will find his right parents. I'm sure of it.'

We were met at Hangzhou airport by our new guide, Jimmy, who was a Chinese version of John Denver, the spit in every way. Except that Jimmy behaved exactly like Leslie, our guide in Changsha three years previously. He seemed preoccupied with getting out of the airport rapidly and was anxious to impress us as 'educated elite'. He was a well-meaning fool, like Leslie, and also like Leslie, he was quite unable to inspire the trust or respect he wished from foreigners. Irritating when you're tired: "What did you major in?" is the question repeated by these naively snobbish, ambitious twenty-something guides. The temptation to be facetious is compelling.

In his anxiety to navigate us out of the airport to a waiting taxi Jimmy ran desperately to an escalator as though he was trying to escape a fire. We struggled to keep up; I was pushing a tired, floppy Chung Chung in the buggy and dragging an enormous suitcase on its wheels behind me. O was pushing a heavily laden airport trolley with one hand and pulling a suitcase with the other. In his wild state Jimmy pointed to the escalator expecting us to throw ourselves and our luggage, and our child to its mercy. We refused, suggesting that the lift would be more efficient; yes, yes, he nodded violently, and bolted in search of a lift. We called him back with a strong feeling of Leslie-flavoured déja vu. We were standing by a lift, though it was mostly glass and chrome.

Jimmy did not know the airport very well. "Ah!" Jimmy exclaimed in the taxi afterwards, "da new airpor iss ony thlee munss or!" He seemed to imply that the lift had been at fault for being unexpectedly transparent. O asked him (without expecting an answer) when had he last collected anyone from the new airport. It was very difficult to understand Jimmy's English because he was overly confident and spoke too fast. He had, he informed us proudly, "Majored' in English". I speculated on the effect of mentioning that we hadn't. From his chatter I formed the impression that Jimmy knew very little about the formal adoption process, or that at least he was rusty. I felt that he was talking fast to disguise his panic and to reassure us with his knowledge. "Your behbeh - boy iss i'? He iss impashun waiting for you! He las you areddy!"

I sat deep into the upholstery in the back seat of the taxi as it hurtled along an American-style freeway. I was already giddy from the modern preoccupation, if not obsession, of the young men and women to excel and not to lose face. I resigned myself to another Leslie experience. I contemplated the cultivated scenery fly past in wide, flat, luxuriant rows while O struggled to get to know Jimmy.

The drive was a visual shock. The road was clean, empty, wide and brand new. Tall, brightly coloured houses topped with pagoda roofs blurred past, each one with a large plot of land growing an abundance of leafy green vegetables. Neat row after row of lettuces and cabbages sped by us, but they looked exotic to me in the shrill sunshine, gloriously large and verdant-green. The usual signs of Chinese habitation - washing lines - decorated the buildings, but I was intrigued that there were not as many as there would normally be, nor were they hung as eccentrically as usual. We had both assumed the tall houses to be tenements: why were there not hundreds of lines everywhere? Jimmy proudly explained that they were 'family houses', built on the traditional lines of a ground floor for storage, a balcony floor above with living space - this is where the washing is generally draped - and a pagoda roof ontop. But these modern versions, these tower villas, had added four or five more living space levels in between, finished with a less steep pagoda roof and a roof vent for drawing cooling air down a shaft into the building. All of these bizarrely tall villas were painted in pastel pinks, greens, blues and yellows and all had satellite dishes pointing in every direction. Some houses were more opulent than others, taller and with tinted windows which glinted unpleasantly in the sun. Some were covered in decorative tiles, the Chinese equivalent to coach lamps. We felt as though we had landed in an indigenous theme park or in Toyland. The inhabitants of the outer limits of Hangzhou were doing O.K. it seemed. We shouted to Jimmy against the wind in the taxi. "The place looks rich, comfortable..." "Thank you!" he shouted into the wind, beaming under his John Denver glasses at our unintentional praise.

We arrived at the Hotel Wanghu at twelve-thirty p.m. As I took in the geography of yet another grand and granited hotel foyer Jimmy told us hurriedly with a fixed, frightened grin, that we need only meet him back here at five minutes to two. He held his belly, pretending to laugh, "Your apoinman at regist awffice issa twoclar, anna za bauding issa cross roar. Vay funny!"

It took time to check in, bring all our gear up to our new room and order room service. I was spinning from plane-and-taxi-momentum, I was hungry and I was deeply tired. We compared notes and decided that the registration must be happening at two o'clock (after the required one hour for lunch in government buildings in China when everything stops and silence rules) so the office must be very close. Unless Jimmy runs everywhere; he seemed to. Autopilot sent me digging into our cases for baby stuff but there was nothing except one small pair of trousers and a T-shirt. Everything else we had brought with us for Ping Ping had gone back with him. I surveyed our stuff strewn all over the room. O noticed the time. We were about to start our comfort food of omelettes and chips. We had fifteen minutes to eat, wash the travelling out, clear ourselves of the events of the last six days and prepare to meet Hua Hua.

The registry office *was* across the road, a very busy main thoroughfare through 'old' Hangzhou. It could take all day to cross, if you were used to the etiquette of British streets. Finally we had to run very fast behind Jimmy weaving across the road dodging the cars and bicycles, otherwise we could have been uncomfortably late for the registration office.

It was, O said, similar to the children's hospital in Changsha, though much less poor. It was a simple, white building on four floors, each floor with blue blinds at the windows. I thought it looked a bit seaside-y. We walked past a concierge, a smiling man who was watering a pot of bamboo, and into a dark, open stone stairwell, the brick red paint of the dado peeled and faded. Jimmy ran up the steps ahead of us, calling down, the alarm in his voice echoing around the staircase that they would be there now, waiting for us.

We did find them waiting at a very large polished teak table in the Registration office on the second floor; a young man in a suit we presumed to be the orphanage Director, a very beautiful middle-aged woman with wavy hair pinned into a big slide (she could have been Portuguese or South American) and a small figure on her lap wearing a mustard-coloured, crocheted, peaked cap. Their presence in the room was calm, quiet, peaceful. They laughed occasionally at the baby. I thought of Mr Yu; he had been smoking tensely.

The baby was big compared with Ping Ping and serious. His eyebrows

84

indented into his soft forehead into two deeply drawn, tight arabesques, just like the photographs of him at eight months; he was now fourteen-and-a-bit months. I could just see his big, burning red cheeks under that cap, and a dark, glittering look to his averted eyes. I didn't approach him because I felt he needed to stay on the beautiful carer's lap while he observed us. He regarded us warily, these strange people, although he never once looked directly at us; he gazed, penetratingly, and then looked away just in time when we returned his look.

I too, had a lot to take in, and about Hua Hua I reflected immediately; he reminded me of the little boys I went to school with in the nineteen sixties who had short, shaved haircuts, bow ties on special occasions, grubby red cheeks, and jumpers in green, white and brown patterns. He was padded-up like all the babies in China, but he wore as a top layer a Woolworth's jumper so common in my own childhood that I was momentarily transported. I was entranced by the thought that a jumper could reassure me the way this one did.

Hua Hua's beautiful carer beckoned to Chung Chung to come over and meet the baby. She slid, apprehensively, slowly, holding on tight to Zed Zed, arms leading first across an expanse of polished teak. I glanced around the room; the table and chairs took up most of the space and beneath them, unseen and neglected, the carpet was filthy. At one end of the room was a long, smaller table. Behind it hung a red Chinese flag and above it on the wall was a shiny red and gold circular shield depicting the tomb of Mao surrounded by five stars and a sun rising from the gold swagged border. Next to this on the wall were large Chinese characters boldly marking the wall horizontally in red plastic. I didn't ask Jimmy about them. I wanted to keep things simple.

Chung Chung stood in front of Hua Hua looking at him. He looked away, uncomfortable at the scrutiny. The beautiful carer bounced him fast on her knees, talking to him, laughing gently. He wouldn't turn back, apparently absorbed in something interesting in a dark corner. Jimmy introduced us to the Director of the orphanage and we sat down shyly opposite him at the large table. He gave us his card: Fuyang Social Welfare Center Hangzhou Zhejiang, Sheng Yong Gan, Director. Through Jimmy we shared pleasantries, not sure when the formalities would begin. He asked us why our adoption of Hua Hua was so sudden: like us he had known only the day before. While we told him a little about Ping Ping we regarded Hua Hua from a distance. Poor little Hua Hua, he had no idea at all what was happening to him.

A young woman bustled in slowly. She was heavily pregnant, and though

85

she was obviously quick by nature, nature was slowing her down. She had the usual thin pencilled eyebrows and a very pale, economical and open, flat face. She seemed to be wearing a tailored sack held up by thin shoulder straps. Underneath it she wore a thick black jumper decorated with zips which looked like diamante snail trails and a diamante teddy on a thin chain around the neck of the jumper. Her English was exceptionally good, but it was drowned in a thick accent and became so unrecognizable in the speed of her delivery that we had to concentrate hard to understand her. I felt my eyebrows twisting with the effort, like Hua Hua's.

We needed to have everything concerning the adoption, including security approval from the Police and the Chinese passport from the Notary, stamped, double stamped and finalised by the end of the day. Even with Jimmy I felt this was possible now I had seen our highly efficient Registrar, though I was beginning to feel the heat seeping in through the open window. Jimmy was wearing a thick jumper under a thick jacket, Hua Hua had his jumper on, the Registrar had her diamante jumper on, the director wore a suit and tie, and the beautiful carer had her coat buttoned up to her neck. The beautiful carer looked hard at Chung Chung's clothes: trousers and a light cotton polo-neck. She asked politely through Jimmy if Chung Chung was warm enough. We laughed. I wondered why they were not all yawning under their thick layers in the torpid heat. She giggled with embarrassment. She must have met many westerners who also did not dress sensibly.

The Registrar moved away to officiate over another adoption and a thin deputy in regulation pond brown suit and jumper came in with handfulls of forms. We began filling them in; our names, ages, signatures, reasons for wanting Hua Hua, our promise never to abandon him... and we asked questions about the baby. I was surprised to hear through Jimmy what the beautiful carer was saying. She described an ordinary routine for a bottle-fed baby: a poo on waking, one and a half bottles of rice powder and milk between six and seven in the morning for breakfast, one bottle of mashed rice and milk for lunch at ten-ish, followed by a sleep, milk and rusks at three for tea, play until supper (as lunch), at five, play until bedtime at eight. A pee ten minutes after each meal and sleeping on his back. I was impressed by the simplicity of this routine and the complete lack of falsehood about her description of it; no vegetables or meat came into his diet obviously, and she didn't feel it was required of her to invent them. I liked her more and more. I could see, now that she had taken his cap off, that the baby certainly did sleep on his back, for his head seemed to be quite flat, following a line vertically upwards from the back of his neck. I reflected on the baby's admirable digestive system too, and wondered at its order. Institutions are not so bad in some ways, I thought.

86

We asked Mr Sheng how far away Fuyang was. He smiled. "One hour by van," he said, "and one hour back... How far away is London?" he asked with an ironic smile. We smiled too. O asked him why he was working as Director of the orphanage. He explained that he and many millions of students learn administration and business management at universities across China and that their courses are paid for by the State. As payment against these loans or grants, the state requires the graduates to take on administration work for public institutions, such as hospitals, schools and orphanages. He was disarmingly open about his indifference to his current job; he had ambitions for bigger things. I liked his honesty very much. I now liked him as much as I liked her. Hua Hua has been looked after by honest, genuine people, I thought, and although they live and work in the rough countryside, they are not hardened people.

Gradually the room began to fill with people. The orphanage driver came in and settled in a chair in a corner, grinning and winking at Hua Hua intermittently. More registration officials came in with a young, thin American couple who sat against a wall looking pale and angry. They sat apart, staring ahead while a little girl of about six hopped and skipped about. Jimmy said he overheard their guide explaining to the Registrar that the little girl didn't like the American couple and wanted to come home. She was playing with her carer, very happily. The distress of the couple was an uncomfortable sight; a reminder that these children *are* Chinese and that we are removing them from what they know. I looked at Chung Chung flirting with Hua Hua's carer; she didn't remember her orphanage. I watched Hua Hua avoiding eye-contact and feigning interest in an empty corner; I felt that he might take a while longer to get used to us than Chung Chung did.

The beautiful carer went outside for some water, leaving Hua Hua on Mr Sheng's lap. Hua Hua turned pink and bellowed loudly. Mr Sheng laughed and tried to cradle him in his arms. Hua Hua struggled furiously and noisily, his big tears crashing and rolling over Mr Sheng's suit. The driver reached for the bottle of milk and offered it to Hua Hua. The baby yelled more. Mr Sheng struggled to make Hua Hua drink. We laughed. So did he. When the carer returned she pretended to be horrified to see him trying - and failing - so hopelessly to feed the baby. The sight of this 'indifferent' man trying to pacify Hua Hua was very funny.

The Registrar came over to us now with more forms to sign: these we had to swear to, by God. This we did, nervously. She signalled to the beautiful carer that Hua Hua's footprint was needed. He watched with eyebrows knotting in concentration as the carer took his shoe and sock off and the

Registrar placed his foot firmly on a pad of red ink and then pressed it precisely onto a sheet of paper. Mr Sheng stood up and shook our hands, the beautiful carer carried the half-shod Hua Hua in our direction and the Registrar smiled. "Congratulations", she said, pressing a little panda into Hua Hua's hands, "I hope you will all be very happy". Yes, thank you! we gestured, forgetting the sad American couple, thank you!

Without further thought I precipitated down the stone steps after the scurrying Jimmy, following his unexplained hurry. O was behind me, carrying Hua Hua - who was astonished into silence - and Chung Chung came last, triumphantly clutching the panda. I can remember the sound of our feet, now, on the stone flags, echoing in the stairwell, and the sense of breathless urgency as we self-propelled, en masse, past the bemused concierge who was still pottering around his small territory.

We followed Jimmy through the streets of old Hangzhou at a canter, breaking into a gallop when we lost him round a corner. The place was reminiscent of British seaside resorts in the early nineteen sixties. A multitude of sweet shops, cook shop stalls, hairdressers and camera shops squeezed tightly along the thoroughfare which ribbonned along the east side of West Lake. I was sure he was taking us around in circles because we seemed to pass the same bookshop several times. It was not easy; the pavements were rocky and dangerously pot-holed and there was a foul stink in those streets which glued itself to the nostrils. O and I took it in turns to carry Hua Hua and now Chung Chung, who had become tortoise-like with tiredness. Hua Hua was only little, but he carried awkwardly in my arms and he did not know about holding on. When I carried him his head obscured my view; our excursion had become so feverish that I scrambled on blindly anyway, aware that I could fall down a pot-hole, trip over a raised cobble, or walk into a stationary bicycle at any moment.

Jimmy darted into a small photograper's shop without warning. It was tiny and we stood in a huddle. Jimmy said something very fast. The young men in the shop lugubriously rose from their board game and set up an umbrella and a stool under it, motioning for us to sit down and smile. We settled in front of a sky blue paper cloth and smiled. Hua Hua screamed in his Woolworth's jumper. He screamed and screamed. He went pink. Real tears squeezed out, rolling onto my hand. The third attempt worked; when the flash blew Hua Hua looked away, but this time he was not terrified. Chung Chung felt excluded so we posed again, awkwardly, with all of us sharing one little stool and trying to look relaxed. This time as the bulb flashed Hua Hua regarded the camera calmly, Chung Chung and O smiled delightfully and I looked away with my eyes crossed.

I understood, very late, that we were taking pictures for the Notary. These had not been necessary for Chung Chung's adoption in 1998, and for Ping Ping's adoption the photographer had a small studio in the new teak-panelled Registration office in Changsha. Jimmy rushed us off again, haring around more streets, past more cakeshops, bookshops, bicycles, and congee and noodle stalls. The sour stench was intense. Whenever it was my turn to carry Hua Hua the smell became worse. I realised that he was reeking of the same pungent stink, a stink so disgusting to my senses that when I carried him my face involuntarily crumpled.

We came to a sudden stop behind Jimmy and fell into another photography shop. This time we had to follow Jimmy up a narrow flight of steep stairs. At the top, there was a small shop-cum-studio with no one apparently in it. Jimmy disappeared into a side room for some time and tumbled out explosively beckoning for one of us to take Hua Hua up an even steeper, ricketier set of stairs. Hua Hua had his photograph taken alone with two gentlemen who, I hope, were used to screamers.

We returned to the Registry office with the photographs, and a triumphant Jimmy far ahead in the lead. We saw the beaten-up black Volkswagen van belonging to the Fuyang orphanage in the car park and realised that Mr Sheng, the beautiful carer, and the driver were waiting for us to finalise the adoption process. I thought we were to return to the office to do this, but Jimmy bolted off again, and we obviously had to follow.

Our walk to the Zhejiang Public Notary Office was shorter along the main old Hangzhou thoroughfare, but it was just as fraught with obstacles and snares. The building itself was new and nondescript, with green tinted windows to keep out the hot east China sun, much like our hotel Wunghu. We followed Jimmy into an efficient, highly organised office, where all the important people, notably women, wore uniform. They looked like 'top brass' police, their square black serge shoulders decorated with stripes and badges of status and achievement. We were told to go upstairs where we waited in a room around another polished teak boardroom table. A young woman walked into the room in full uniform and peaked cap circled with striped ribbon. Jimmy greeted her enthusiastically as though he was the 'proud father', shaking her hand vigorously. I watched, fascinated. She was tall, slim and incredibly good-looking, even more wonderful than Stella. I felt grubby by then and I was embarrassed to shake the hand of someone so perfect.

More signing, more swearing by the Bible (Chinese officialdom seems to assume that because Britain is a church state then it follows that all British citizens share one 'state' belief), and more stamping of a highly important

89

kind, judging by the seriousness of the Notary and the obsequiousness of Jimmy. That done, we moved off again, this time lumbering fast back to the Registration office where we were shoved straight into the Fuyang van. I was still standing when the van took off briskly, squealing as it turned out of the gates. O sat near to Jimmy towards the front of the van and managed to ask him where we were going now. "Security!" he shouted, excitedly, "the Police Station! They close at five o'clock!"

I sat in the back of the van with Hua Hua on my lap trying to catch my breath. It was 4.45 p.m. and it was hot and close. We needed to request permission for Hua Hua to leave the country and to get Security authorisation of his Chinese passport from the Police station on the same day as the registration and the notarisation of the adoption itself. Mr Sheng, as ex-guardian, needed to be included in the formalities. We had a quarter of an hour to get there and lodge the applications. We could collect the passport and the other documents another day but the application had to be 'live' on adoption day. The elderly van drove wildly round the old Hangzhou streets; we had to hold on to the seats in front when it cornered, to avoid being thrown across onto each others' laps.

I felt that I should take the jumper off Hua Hua now; he would have adjusted to the notion that a change of personnel was taking place, so he wouldn't be so shocked now at losing his hot, outer layer. He was sleepy and he seemed to be happy with me. The jumper pulled off easily. He was wearing a bright red cotton quilted jacket as the next under-layer. It was hand-sewn with very small, regular stitches with a nineteen fifties' design fabric and finished with cardboard buttons which had been painted black and varnished. I fell in love with the jacket; it was beautiful, it was original, and it belonged to Hua Hua. Amazingly this baby, with his dancing eyebrows which seemed exclusively to express his feelings - and were therefore the windows to his soul, I felt - fell asleep on my lap in the van as it swerved hysterically around the Hangzhou streets. I fell in love with him, too.

The van mounted the pavement at speed along a narrow street and stopped suddenly outside an imposing police station. It looked like a central post office in Paris in the nineteen fifties: the floor was black polished granite, and running across three sides of the hall was a shoulder-high counter dotted with pot plants and supported by slender columns of deep red Formica in a marble design. Police men and women stood behind the high counters in their military-style uniforms but they seemed, like me, to be struggling to see over the top of the counter and through the decorative greenery.

Jimmy called out for service with a nervous, ingratiating grin. O got out our paperwork from his briefcase with one hand while Chung Chung held on to his other hand. Mr Sheng prepared all his papers, too, while the beautiful carer and the driver were present as formal witnesses. I tried to take part in the event and hovered behind Jimmy while I carried the sleepy Hua Hua. With one hand Jimmy was clinging on to the counter talking excitedly while he gesticulated with the other to a young policeman. I was too soggy now to take part in the formalities, nor to understand them. I was happy to just watch and dream, but I couldn't see much really, apart from the red counter fascia and their backs. The policeman asked for the photographs. Jimmy panicked, and like the best man at a wedding, frantically searched through all his pockets. There was a sudden movement, a rush of bodies in my direction and the sound of 'aaaar!' from the policeman, from Mr Sheng, the beautiful carer, the driver, O, and from Jimmy who made the biggest lunge and the loudest shout. A strappy-leaved fern in a shiny silver pot had been dislodged by one of Jimmy's panicking arms and was flying towards Hua Hua and me. I saw their faces momentarily - with expressions of horror and surprise - watch the thing as it flew through the air while gravity began to separate plant from pot. Jimmy caught it before it hit the ground, stuffed the plant and the spilled earth hurriedly back into the pot and almost threw it back onto the high counter. I took Hua Hua to sit on benches by the large windows which looked on to the narrow street. We watched from a distance as Jimmy breathed deeply and found the photographs in his breast pocket. The police station remained open for us until the paperwork was over.

We returned in the van to our Hotel foyer, where the creamy marble, the bellboys, the big white sofas and the polished brass all came as a shock after our afternoon of administration offices, treacherous pavements and lakeside photographers. We agreed that I would take Hua Hua up to our room for us to decompress while O and Chung Chung handed over the donation money to Mr Sheng downstairs. I shook hands with Mr Sheng and the beautiful carer. In a state of tired and exhilarated abandon I ignored my lack of Chinese and their lack of English and thanked them enthusiastically, knowing that those good people would certainly understand me very well.

I drifted up with Hua Hua in the lift, this time with no energy to spare on lift anxiety; "Now", I wondered aloud, looking at us both in the mirrors which surrounded us on three sides, "how are we together?"

It is ironic to me now, given that we had a stills camera and a video camera with us, that O and I took so few photographs and filmed so little during these momentous days. We have a few pictures of Ping Ping's last minutes with us in Changsha but it hurts me to look at them. I gave Hua Hua's splendid mustard crocheted peaked cap back to Fuyang orphanage, thinking that it would be more useful there; we didn't even think of taking a picture of Hua Hua in it. At crucial moments life takes over. I can't live the moment *and* record it. I dream with nostalgia of that non-existent picture of Hua Hua in his mustard, crocheted, peaked cap.

We had a small amount of whiskey left from our stores of St Patrick's day Jamieson and an unopened packet of McVities digestive biscuits which O had bought - how inspired! - from the up-market 'food-store' at Beijing airport. I looked helplessly into the refrigerated mini-bar for something baby-friendly, and at the tea-making station, spotlit as usual, and supplied with a 'smart-thermos': a very large thermos kettle which constantly brought water up to the required tea-making temperature, so dispensing with the knock on the door followed by an anonymous hand holding a fresh hot thermos. Apart from green jasmine tea, sugar or water from the tea-making station, it was clear what Hua Hua was going to try: I put him on the bed, in the middle, and offered him a sweet, buttery, crumbly digestive biscuit. His hands didn't move, and he looked at me by a sideways glance, curious and shy. I put the biscuit into his hand and moved his hand and the biscuit to his mouth. The sensation of the thing in his hand and on his lip then activated an interest in him; he tried, tentatively, to put the biscuit to his mouth. I perched on the edge of the bed watching him. I didn't want to frighten him by getting too close, but at the same time I didn't want him to feel lost in this strange place with me, still a stranger.

O came in without Chung Chung in a rush to say he was going out with Jimmy and Chung Chung to buy supplies. What did we need? We ran through an improvised list - why had we not thought of this in Beijing? - covering everything from nappies to pyjamas to milk and feeding bottles: the basic kit in other words...everything we had sent to Ping Jiang.

O: 'It was after six p.m. and night had fallen when Chung Chung and I confidently followed Jimmy out of the hotel on a mission to buy a bottle, some powdered milk, some nappies and some pyjamas for Hua Hua. I assumed that he would take us to a local supermarket nearby, but Jimmy had decided (rashly and without mentioning it to us) to make an outing of it to a newly opened grand department store. He must have been more concerned to impress me than to help me - a tired and very drained forty one year old - and so made us walk for twenty minutes to it. The new store was smart and expensive; clearly this was Jimmy's first visit too and he was anxious to see inside so he whisked us to the most expensive department displaying all the western designer and couture labels. We did not see any Gucci pyjamas for infants or Calvin Klein nappies... On another floor we found some pyjamas, made in Japan, and a bath thermometer Chung Chung fell for. Jimmy suddenly announced "No food in department store!" and insisted we follow him out to another shop where he was sure to find food.

I had so much admiration for the way Chung Chung was coping with all these events, but she was nearly four years old and understandably she was becoming tired; now I carried Chung Chung to our next destination, one that Jimmy promised was not too far.

We walked for another twenty minutes and I became disoriented, having completely lost my sense of direction. It was after seven p.m. when we found a cramped supermarket in the basement of an office block built in the nineteen twenties. It was there that we found baby food and nappies for Hua Hua and crisps and juice for a deserving Chung Chung. Now very tired and hungry and still carrying Chung Chung I walked with Jimmy a long way back to the hotel. Later, the following day I found a large, well-stocked supermarket next to our hotel...'

Hua Hua and I continued to watch each other quietly and to feel our way to making contact again. I sat down on the edge of the bed again with the second to last generous measure of whiskey. We stayed like this for some time: Hua Hua was now enjoying sucking the biscuit and was dribbling steadily. I was beginning to sense that O and Chung Chung were out on a bigger errand than I had first imagined. I was longing to unlace his tight yellow nylon boots to let his feet breathe and his toes wriggle; I had to wait, I had to give him time in his clothes, while their smell and sensation could give him comfort...

As I turned the corner to go into the bathroom Hua Hua shrieked. I sprang back in alarm, thinking that in those few seconds something dreadful must have happened. I sat on the bed again, searching his face for signs of distress. He smiled at me, and for the first time he looked directly at me. I gave him another biscuit, I suppose as a prize. I was anxious, too, to provide comfort for him from a bit of distance; I reasoned to myself that if he wasn't used to being cuddled, this was the wrong moment to start, and food was the ultimate comfort. I turned the corner again into the bathroom. Another terrifying shriek came from this little being. I rushed to him again. He smiled at me, almost flirtatiously, and took a big bite of soggy biscuit.

Slowly, I took Hua Hua's boots off: I was struck by their message emblazoned in red; 'Dang Beng, Baby Hoes' and the rim of soft yellow synthetic fur at the ankles. His socks were of electric blue nylon, stiff with age, and his overtrousers, with the open gap for putting on and taking off nappies were lemon yellow and quilted, like fluffy lemon mousse, with a lining which repeated, in jolly script, 'Fashion!'. His undertrousers were, like Chung Chung's had been, grey with old sweat and lack of washing. Underneath his jacket with the varnished buttons, as a vest he wore a thick red long-sleeved sweatshirt, a garment we in the west would wear as a jumper. His skin was dull, grey and dusty. The year of sweating he had spent under these hot layers had cooked the dirt into his skin. I let Hua Hua stay grubby, but so that he could cool off I dressed him in the little soft trousers and T-shirt we had first dressed Chung Chung in.

Hua Hua was sitting up without help but his legs were very weak and bowed, curling too readily into the crossed-legged position. I wondered, with a dash of disappointment, if this baby had spent much of his time sitting in that dormitory cot, whereas - though she too had been as grubby when we collected her - Chung Chung had been building up to her first steps.

I went into the bathroom again to give his clothes a light wash. again the baby shrieked and I returned to sit on the bed with a new glass of whiskey and another digestive biscuit. We played on the bed with the paper coasters from the tea-making corner and the complimentary hotel stationary and laundry lists. I tried giving him a sip of water from a small cup but the water cascaded down his chin and into his lap; "a bottle-only baby, then," I said to him, "and we have no bottles!" He smiled wetly and broadly.

It felt that O and Chung Chung had been away for a long time. I imagined that they must have been having a grand time at the shops. It was becoming increasingly difficult to improvise with digestive biscuits and stationery. I now badly needed a pee, but I felt unable to leave Hua Hua alone on the bed, even for a second.

I used the time to draw Hua Hua for a fax I wanted to send to London: an announcement...'Friday 23rd March from the Stockman family, including Louis Hua Hua Buster Jijun Stockman, born 02.01.2000.' I had drawn an elf with curled, arched brows, dirty round cheeks and two little front teeth.

When O and Chung Chung returned with nappies, bottles, pyjamas, rusks and a bath thermometer shaped as a pink blob they were both very tired. O had lost patience with Jimmy who had taken them on an unnecessarily long and twisted cross-town hike. Most of the things, I noted with interest, were not actually made in China, but in Japan. Odd for us, given the huge importing of goods into Britain from China. One of the powdered baby milks they had bought on their outing was a shiny red box of sachets containing the measured amount of powder for one full bottle, a sort of 'camping' baby milk for improvisers. I was very taken with this invention and by its name: *Beingmate*.

O also brought with him the rest of the paperwork from Mr Sheng: a red satin book stating that the adoption took place on the twenty-third of March 2001 and who we are and who Hua Hua is, using his 'new' name, also with official stamps; a brown leatherette book containing our names and address with, again, official stamps; the photograph of us with a disconsolate baby in a Woolworth's jumper on our lap; and then three photographs in a rice paper envelope of the orphanage in Baigian Village, Luzhu Town near Fuyang. The building looked neat and clean, with a recognisable economy about it, clipped bushes and no sign of peeling paint on the gate post walls...and unusually, not even a leaning bicycle.

The photographs of Hua Hua were interesting. They were companions of the photograph we were given at the CCAA. Now I was better able to read more into the pictures. Hua Hua was outside on a bamboo mat on the grass under a low tree. He was pulling his head up to see the camera, but his legs behind him looked very floppy, much like a young baby's. The date on the pictures showed he was eight months old. Amongst the set was a more revealing picture of Hua Hua in his cot in a dormitory. In the same vest of little pink roses - the pictures of Hua Hua as a baby were taken on that same day - Hua Hua held the same position, only holding himself up by the arms and looking at the camera. The cot was bare except for the mat, a rolled-up towel, and a teddy which was tied to the ends of his and the adjoining cot, presumably for sharing. A bleak view for a growing baby. I understood now why he yelled for me whenever I was out of sight; yelling must have been his only strategy in the orphanage and he was continuing what he felt to be an effective way to make contact with people and to keep it.

It was a little more than that, we realised later, when we couldn't get Hua Hua to look at O. Hua Hua was also frightened of unknown men and refused to acknowledge them. He was more open to women, especially middle-aged ones with big smiles for him. We assumed that, as for most children in the orphanages, only women had cared for him. He seemed to be particularly affected by it: he was terribly shy.

We raided the new supplies for something tempting for Chung Chung and Hua Hua. We ignored our usual fear and outrage at the prices and raided the mini-bar for ourselves.

I still needed a pee but now I was apprehensive about using the loo. It was a computerized piece of plumbing, an unpredictable animal. The avocado-coloured lavatory itself was conventional, though very low on the ground, and it had what looked like an armrest at the side with instructions and symbols with press-buttons under a plastic cover. I was nervous about standing near it in case, sensing my presence, it wanted to throw water at me. What it did do, I learnt later, after O had studied it with great interest, was to wash and blow-dry you afterwards, depending on what you had programmed it to do, and therefore what you had used it for. Although, of course these two actions may not be linked. I avoided it. O and Chung Chung used it a lot.

A shy, grinning girl knocked on the door to make up Chung Chung's truckle bed. O teased her in the nicest way. Hua Hua remained cross-legged in the centre of the bed ignoring her little claps and smiles. Another girl came in to make up Hua Hua's cot with layers of white puffy squares. O teased her, too. Room service came in also, with plates of fried rice for us and congee for Hua Hua. I half-expected Groucho Marx to knock on the door offering manicures.

We called home to London and struggled to describe the delights and idiosyncrasies of baby Hua Hua to people who had been agonising on our behalf and preparing to welcome home a grief-stricken family.

I climbed into bed in gratitude to those laundry girls who haunt the corridors of each floor of the hotel making beds, cleaning the rooms, collecting the laundry and delivering room service meals. They don't go out anywhere, but live their lives in the corridors and rooms-off. They are probably married, and they probably have children. But we, temporary, transient and unknown to them, are their life.

Chung Chung, O and Hua Hua slept soundly all night. I spent much of the night listening to Hua Hua's breathing. At times he snored loudly, at others he was totally silent; at those times I got up to watch the bedclothes move.

Saturday 24th March, Hotel Wanghu, Hangzhou

The view from the picture windows on the sixth floor breakfast area covered a vast expanse of West Lake: *'Melting Snow at Broken Bridge'*, *'Autumn Moon on Calm Lake'*, *'Diamond Hill under the Evening Sun'*, *'The Tomb and Temple of Yuefei'*, *'Lotus in the Breeze at Crooked Courtyard'*, *'Spring Dawn at Su Causeway'* and *'Three Pools Mirroring the Moon'*. We couldn't see any of it; a mist had settled over West Lake some days ago, and despite the shards of sun which forced themselves through the clouds, it didn't look as though the cold, grey mist was going to lift.

The breakfast floor had been furnished with the American Deep South in mind. Reproduction four-seater leather Chesterfield sofas were pulled up tightly to dark, mahogany tables laid with thick white linen napkins and lines of shiny hotel cutlery. Our choice was a little more gentle this time; cornflakes, scrambled eggs and do-it-yourself toast with stale buns, congee, those hard beans, and chicken feet in hot spicy sauce under a silver lid. What was different here was the freshly squeezed orange juice in a machine, which we coyly put our glasses to many times, feeling that we might be exploiting the situation.

O had an appointment with Jimmy early at the police station to collect Hua Hua's passport and his adoption papers. The most important of the documents, his permission to leave the country, would be ready for us on Tuesday morning. He took Chung Chung with him. I stayed in the hotel room with Hua Hua who played contentedly with postcards, and complimentary toothbrushes and combs, while I pottered about playing with him, washing some clothes, re-arranging our luggage and reading out loud, longingly, about West Lake on a clear day.

We returned to "our" table for lunch. The mist hung denser and greyer; from the sixth floor picture window Hangzhou was reduced to a busy road junction with no evidence of a lake, or a view across it. We watched the intricate agitations and crossings of pedestrians, vans, bicycles and cars. There was a mutually understood code amongst these teeming inhabitants of Hangzhou which seemed to have no relation at all to the traffic lights.

Fate had sent us the long way round, across twelve thousand miles of sea, desert, peasant countryside, and grim conurbations, to a celebrated national holiday resort to observe (fascinated nevertheless) ordinary human behaviour at a town junction on a Saturday morning.

Apart from receiving and sending faxes from the 'Business Bureau' in the hotel to deal with problems with the film at home, O now had to deal with the travel arrangements, too. He needed to go with Chung Chung to the ticket office of China Eastern Airlines in order to buy four seats for us to fly from Shanghai to London. Having got Hua Hua's visa for entry into the UK from the British consulate in Shanghai there would be no need to return to Beijing. Our Beijing to London return flight needed to be cancelled and we were hoping to transfer the cost, since we were now very low on funds.

It was very difficult for O to explain to the young women at the ticket office that - through BLAS - we had already paid for our train to Shanghai and for one night's stay in a hotel there. In order to make the reservation they needed to know all our names; in the rush of Hua Hua's adoption we had not been shown how to write Hua Hua's first name, "Jijun", in Pinyin (the phonetic translation into the western alphabet) or in Chinese. O was at a loss. He wrote variations on the back of an envelope. The astonishing, and also depressing, thing is that the clerks accepted all his wrong attempts, without comment and without interest. I have kept the envelope as a souvenir, a little sweet and a little sour; a scrap which tells so much about our struggles with the obscure, intimate depths of the Chinese way; officialdom and the bleak disinterest of the multitude.

While O and Chung Chung were out on this mission Hua Hua slept, surrounded by plumped pillows and half-chewed paper coasters. I wrote a fax to our lady at the Department of Health. I had now lost my sense of time and date;

'Room 223 Wanghu Hotel, Hangzhou, Zhejiang Province, China.
Friday March 23rd 2001. 2.45 a.m.

Dear Christine,
We left Changsha early, returned to Beijing in the belief that we would go home to London, to recover and to regroup! Yesterday we saw the deputy Director of the CCAA at the offices just to tell them what happened. They encouraged us to stay and adopt a third child. In 24 hours we have come full-circle. We are now back in the South, near Shanghai, and have a strapping 14-month-old boy in rude health. We are all jolly tired from the extremes of emotion and travelling. Many thanks for your help, love Annabel'

Late in the afternoon we set off for a walk in the rain. For a small sum we hired an umbrella from an eager bellboy in the foyer and set off, purposefully, in the direction of the bookshop we had passed so many times the day before.

I was anticipating this large seaside bookshop to be like the Foreign Languages Bookstore in Beijing - I had developed a taste for bookshops in Beijing on our first trip to collect Chung Chung. This shop of course was much smaller and stocked titles that only Chinese people would be interested in. But I did find something which caught my interest: a *'Medicated Diet of Traditional Chinese Medicine'*. 'Section 3 Purgative Drugs. Honey. EFFICIENCIES; *Nourish the body, moisturize the intestine and relax the bowels, nourish the lung and relieve cough, nourish and strengthen the middle-jiao, alleviate pain, detoxify poisonous effects.* INDICATIONS; *External use for skin infection, burn and skin ulcer.'* I thought about Hua Hua who now had a burning red right cheek which was showing signs of excema-style ulceration and a cough which was moving deeper into his chest. I decided to buy the book and took one last look; 'Section 15 Anthelmintics. Anthelmintics are indicated for diseases caused by parasites in the intestines such as ascariasis, enterobiasis, cestodiasis and ancylostomiasis. Chinese Torreya. INDICATIONS *For ascariasis ad taeniasis, also for constipation due to dryness of intestine. For parasitic infestation: 15-30g (fried) for chewing, or prepared as pill or powder.'* Remembering, with a shudder, that our poor little Chung Chung had been harbouring an ascaris worm, discovered alive by O when she had been with us for a year, I decided that yes, at fourteen yuan, this was a book I was going to refer to, often.

O found a book for Chung Chung: the title, *'Chinese Tale Series'* was written in Chinese and English above a drawing of a handsome Bronze Age couple and their beautiful Bronze Age baby. On each page, above two lines each of English and Chinese script was a large, stylised Chinese drawing - with a modern interpretation - depicting a dramatic moment from the stories 'Hou Yi Shoots the Suns', 'Chang'e Flying to the Moon', 'Shen Nong's Miracle Herbs' and 'Jingwei Filling the Sea'. It cost sixty-five Yuan. It was expensive, but this comic book was Chung Chung's now, her name was written on it, and it was going to be indispensable.

Although eyes were not openly directed at us, we were being observed with deep interest in the crowded shop, and when Hua Hua yelled and wouldn't let go of a cheap westernised pop-up book we reluctantly bought it to get out of the shop quickly. We returned to the hotel in a downpour.

While we waited for a room service supper of fried rice for us and congee for Hua Hua, O called Bernie Connolly at the British Embassy in Beijing to thank her and to let her know what had happened.

That night O read Chung Chung to sleep on her truckle bed with the story of how Hou Yi shot the Suns. By four in the morning Chung Chung was in the big bed with O and I was in the truckle bed, one foot tangling with the handle of a suitcase, the other squashed uncomfortably against the metal frame. Through the ghastly green of the tinted window I could see a glowing moon hanging over Hangzhou. It would have been hanging over the lake, too, glowingly and benignly, I thought wistfully, and I would be able to see it if our window were facing that way.

Sunday 25th March 2001, Hotel Wanghu, Hangzhou

We walked miles around old and new Hangzhou in the morning after breakfast looking for a bank. We needed to withdraw Yuan 12,684 in cash (St. £1,2684) on our credit cards to pay for the air tickets to get back to London. The air was stickily warm and heavy, and a fierce, but opaque brightness illuminated a dense haze which had rolled in from West Lake. I was never going to see what the travel guides describe in ecstatic raptures, and the desire now to return home was beginning to conjure an almost hallucinogenic vision of My Own Bed, Radio Four, and Fresh Hot Coffee.

Hua Hua took to my carrying him in a sling very easily. After initial surprise, he enjoyed the enclosure of it very much. Like a marsupial he curled up, fell asleep, and remained asleep throughout our long walk around town. Chung Chung took to the buggy and stayed in it for the rest of our time in China.

After collecting our tickets from China Eastern Airlines - which included one for "Hua Juijin", O's final much-considered guess - we wandered slowly back to the hotel stopping to look around a few shops. The supermarket was terribly expensive and stocked with high-expectation, brightly coloured, over-packaged consumer stuff. I couldn't imagine Chinese people actually spending their money on these things: across the road they were fighting over very cheap nylon baby-suits for sale from a chaotic encampment of clothes and fabrics of all sizes, patterns and colours. The baby-suits were exactly like the one Chung Chung had been wearing when we first saw her in that silent, sweltering courtyard in Changsha. I was infected by the clamour to buy. I hesitated; should I buy one, for sentiments' sake?

We went into a small CD shop, on the pretext of looking for a CD of traditional Chinese songs for Chung Chung; drawn in, I suppose, by its emptiness and its exaggerated pretensions. The pictures stuck on the window of pop stars and Hollywood actors tried to create an air of excitement, but actually it was those ubiquitous Chinese colours, vermilion red and magenta pink, which hid the fact that everything stacked so carefully was really quite dull, including a CD with a picture of David and Victoria Beckham looking a bit out of date, and entitled "David Beckham Sings"... I should have bought it.

Stepping carefully along the broken-up pavement we found ourselves in familiar territory; that repellant smell of the drains and the cooking of coagulated congee at the food stalls near West Lake lodged itself again into our nostrils. Hurrying on we found the promenade of West Lake on the other side of the bend. It was a wide gravel walk, used by genteel visitors who ambled arm in arm, people-watching. We watched them too, from a bench, trying to guess if they were from the north of China, or Korea or Japan. Full of hope, we watched the white haze over West Lake, too. It remained, in my opinion, obstinately static and unhelpfully there.

After a picnic lunch on the bed in the hotel O and Chung Chung went out for a stroll to find some shops where they could buy more baby supplies and some whiskey for me. Hua Hua was beginning to attach himself to me like glue. It surprised me; I hadn't imagined myself becoming a motherly comfort-figure, even by default. Whenever I moved away, or even turned away from him now, Hua Hua shouted anxiously, so it was a relief to me when he slept that afternoon while I squeezed around him rearranging the chaos in the room.

O: ' After we asked directions at the hotel front desk Chung Chung and I walked in the opposite direction Jimmy had taken us two days ago. Immediately a busier and poorer city revealed itself to us on the streets behind the hotel, away from West Lake. We looked through the doorways of some small local supermarkets; although it was obvious they had things we wanted I was too shy to go into them. We passed fishmongers and greengrocers where trade was busy; so brisk that I wondered whether these small shops were supplying the restaurants and hotels.

We found ourselves on the corner of a large thoroughfare and outside a large supermarket; here we could wander around inside looking at everything without the need to ask for help. It was immediately noticeable that (unlike the UK) there was very little alcohol and certainly no whiskey. The choice was either a very expensive French brandy or a local rice wine in what looked like vinegar bottles. I bought a bottle of the local drink which later we found so evil-smelling that it was abandoned in the hotel room when we left. Chung Chung and I looked for rice cakes or rusks for Hua Hua, but we found instead a very large assortment of highly sugared biscuits and sweets.

While we waited at the till to pay for the wine we watched two girls operating one of three very noisy machines which banged and let out puffs of smoke at each bang. After each bang a large, sweet puffed-rice cracker appeared and the second girl put the large crackers into polythene bags five at a time, selling them to passers-by from trestle tables on the street. We bought a bag for Chung Chung who found them delicious; when we arrived back at the hotel she had nearly eaten them all.

As we started off back to the hotel we met a stream of hundreds of blue-uniformed teenagers who were leaving school and jumping onto their bicycles. As we waited for them to disperse we noticed an entrance to a park where people were flying kites. We took a detour there.

The small park was full of people. Some were eating, some were strolling with their family or in small groups of friends, but most of them were trying to fly kites. Because of the low mist there was very little wind at all. Except for a few very large kites high in the sky and flown, probably, by very skilled people, most kites were 'flying' as long as their owners were running! Some children were very determined and ran up and down a lot to get their kites airborne. Others got their parents to do the running. Lovers also were trying to fly their kites, and giggling at the absurdity of the struggle.

There was a small wooden pavillion in the park which was selling all sorts of kites, some complex and others made simply from paper and bamboo. A crowd of people who were buying, adjusting, repairing and generally talking kites surrounded it. As we walked closer we could see some people were assembling three-dimensional kites representing birds: the eagle and the raven were both very impressive. Chung Chung wanted to join in the fun so I bought her a very cheap (one yuan) little kite which we easily put together. Chung Chung ran off, like the wind, and her kite flew very well, but like all the others, only as long as she ran! Of course Chung Chung blended in very well with the children and she pressed on bravely when the adults addressed her in Chinese; I was self-conscious because I did not look like the other fathers! Then Chung Chung's kite tangled with another mid-air and the collision brought hers down, broken. She cried at the sight of its torn paper tail. We collected a small crowd of concerned kite-flyers. One man, talking very fast, regarded the kite as one would a wounded bird; he then called out to an elderly seated man who was eating noodles...Soon one noodle was passed over, and after some chewing and kneading with the fingers, it became a sticky paste suitable to repair the paper tail. It worked and Chung Chung was amazed!'

At supper on the sixth floor, with a night-time view of the street lights and shop signs of Hangzhou (and not the shimmering light of the moon gently reflected in the quiet waters of West Lake) we were serenaded by a trio of ladies in long, black cocktail dresses playing famous western classical hits. The eldest of the women beat time and played the 'cello. It was sometimes difficult for her to do both at once; either the rhythm or the 'cello was compromised by her attention to the other. The flautist and the violinist were both younger and had less experience of their instruments and of performance. But they were a joy to us, with their undaunted spirit and oblivion to their awfulness, and I enjoyed all the hits - the Swan, the Blue Danube and the Wedding March - with a relaxed nostalgia: we were going home soon!

Monday 26th March 2001, Hotel Wanghu, Hangzhou

We had one more day to wait in Hangzhou before we could take the train to Shanghai. We were due to collect the last papers from the police station on Tuesday morning. The weather looked better. We assembled a modest picnic: small oranges sold in the streets by women who came in from the surrounding countryside, little cakes O had bought from a cakeshop, apples from breakfast and a miniature back pack of very sweet, brightly coloured 'jellies' O had bought at the supermarket for Chung Chung.

Meandering along the edge of West Lake, we slowly passed the pagoda shaped jetties and the gondoliers loitering by their craft hoping for a fare. A few small boats lurked on the still, pale water and a broken white mist remained above it obscuring the lake; it could have been a pond, were it not for a few glimpses of distant green hills.

We sat on a bench facing the mist. The gondoliers, all wearing pale blue jackets, came over to us, slowly, like cows do, overcome with curiosity and a thrill of fear. We opened our picnic and O began peeling the oranges. Hua Hua sat on his knee watching this, his eyebrows twisting in concentration. One gondolier felt brave, moving in close to us. He muttered, smiling a little and waved in the direction of his boat. We looked up, "No, thank you", we said, hoping the English would disorient him a little, compromise his efforts to make us pay for a cold boat ride. He slunk off, joining the group of men. They laughed, embarrassed, and determined. Another slid towards us, looking away, smiling, as he approached. With his hands in his pockets he studied us hard at close range through thick glasses, his big head looming over us, smiling and bemused. "No thank you!" we responded together, although O laughed and I growled. He retreated too, thwarted and nonplussed. The bravest then trotted over to us, by now as a dare, amused and defiant. I turned the camera on him, focusing on his weak, un-seeing eyes. I felt regret for him at that moment as he remained, caught and stupid, in the camera lens. I cocked the shutter and he moved away, humiliated, finally seen-off by the eye of the camera.

I spent a liberating afternoon walking alone through new Hangzhou to a very large supermarket. The numbers of pedestrians occupying the streets was daunting; I felt brave and foolish to be alone amongst so many. I talked to myself all the way there and back in order to keep some measure of sense in me; the quantity of humanity pouring along pavements, overpasses and underpasses, and massing at junctions made me feel dislocated from myself, floating in their reality.

I bought some irresistibles and a quantity of useful supplies for our train journey to Shanghai; bottles of water, nappies, a baby's bottle and drinking cup for Hua Hua, two sets of decorated children's chopsticks and plastic spoons and O! triumph! a rubber vaccuum bulb with a soft rubber nozzle for extracting mucous from a baby's nose. This piece of apparatus was super-efficient, because it had a soft rather than a hard detachable nozzle. This would not get the British safety mark due to the risk that one might easily blow into, rather than suck from, baby's nose, or worse, lose the nozzle in baby's nose altogether. I tried unsuccessfully to buy some rice cakes, so instead I bought cheap sugared rice biscuits in packaging reminiscent of the nineteen fifties. They contained biscuits so fine and brittle that they were wrapped in many petticoated layers of soft pleated white paper to protect them.

That night we had supper on the sixth floor accompanied by the music of the ladies in black. Occasionally the 'cello slid on the slippery floor of the raised stage and the flute hitched itself uncontrollably into a higher register and the violin sounded as though it had sawdust on its strings, but the ladies were staunch and unflinching in their purpose. I honestly enjoyed their enthusiastic, uneven playing as we feasted on a large, delicious supper and discovered that Hua Hua was in love with oranges.

Tuesday 27th March 2001, Hotel Wanghu, Hangzhou

At breakfast on the sixth floor Hua Hua was more energetic, more confident, more...experimental than he had been up until then. Everything on the smart green tablecloth was spilt at least once; orange juice, coffee, and milk splashed and brimmed into saucers. The waitresses tried to look at him disapprovingly; he responded by carefully, painstakingly, mopping up the ponds with bread rolls.

We tried to scribble a few impressions onto postcards we had bought in Beijing ten days ago, a time so long ago for us now, it seemed as though it had been another, different trip altogether. I didn't know what to say now; some people knew nothing of our time in China, some still only knew about Ping Ping and a few now knew about Hua Hua. It all seemed a bit lame - just as we were preparing to leave Hangzhou - the notion of cheerful, breezy greetings on a tourist postcard. Besides, I had become virtually inarticulate from the intensity of our experiences and I had been unable to write about them in the diary for days.

While O and Chung Chung returned to the police station with Jimmy to collect Hua Hua's stamped authorisations and passport, Hua Hua and I experimented with a long morning of inertia waiting in the hotel garden. We looked up at the blue awnings of the balconies and the up and down repetitions of the glinting, harsh-green windows. The traffic noisily, incessantly circulated, drawn continually back it seemed, to this junction at the garden gates. We sat on a soft mound of grass near a small pond with a weeping willow, and listened sleepily to the sounds of Hangzhou, turning our heads away from the sharp light which penetrated the thick haze.

A woman with her baby took a short cut through the gardens. They approached us in a hurry, the mother agitated, pointing at Hua Hua. As she came nearer I could see that the mother was smiling excitedly, and still pointing at Hua Hua, she demanded to know if Hua Hua was a boy. This offended me on Hua Hua's behalf. I pretended not to understand. She tried again, pointing at Hua Hua's recently shaved hair. I thought he looked pretty and appropriately androgynous for a year-old baby in his red quilted jacket and again, I refused to understand. The woman must have thought I was a fool, and in one impatient gesture, she pulled her baby boy's trousers down to his feet and triumphantly pointed to his small, innocent sex. I was horrified, both at her treatment of her own baby and at her interest in Hua Hua. I couldn't pretend to remain uncomprehending now; I was angry, disappointed, shocked. This was a major city, not the feudal countryside... *wasn't it?*

107

Jimmy did not order a van (as O had requested) to take us and our luggage to Hangzhou station: out of the laziness which came from his lack of understanding, he hailed a taxi outside the hotel and when we pointed out that we could not all squeeze into it, he hailed another. We had no choice; it was this or being late. In the first taxi we stuffed Jimmy and the big pieces of luggage. Jimmy was still talking fast when the surly driver drove away suddenly without warning, leaving a black cloud of exhaust at the hotel steps. We pressed in apologetically around the driver in the second, equally decrepit and elderly taxi. The driver turned round from the trinkets and lucky charms which obscured his view and smiled at us as we squashed in painfully on the back seat. He shouted against the noise of the engine and accelerated suddenly, leaving, no doubt, another deposit on the hotel steps.

For ten minutes we waited anxiously for Jimmy's taxi to join ours at the drop-off rank at Hangzhou station, and then found ourselves quite suddenly with him, standing at the top of the longest escalator in the world inside the noisiest public building in the world. It was pandemonium in the station and the shouting, grey people in shoals, swarms and multitudes poured and overflowed up and down the steep escalators, walkways, staircases and tunnels.

Jimmy bolted onto the down escalator disappearing into a sea of bodies with a lemming-like abandon, failing yet again to appreciate that we had heavy luggage, and this time, two children to carry. We had also picked up some bedraggled, rosy-cheeked beggars who seemed convinced that if they stuck to us determinedly we would give in, handing over big and small change and possibly a western treat of some kind. A gun? I imagined, cynically. Trying to ignore the tenacious and demanding presence of these beggars, we watched - horrified - Jimmy's slow descent to the bottom of the escalator, much like the passage of molten lava down a volcano, I thought uncharitably. He must have assumed that we were behind him and he didn't look back.

O shouted to me that I would have to stay at the top with the children while he took the bags down the escalator one at a time. Jimmy would have to mind them at the bottom. He launched the biggest suitcase onto the escalator amongst a crowd of people; he was beyond caring about politeness now: we both were. I was anxious about us being separated in this deafening multitude. I was sickened at the thought, also, that the beggars might try to steal Chung Chung or Hua Hua for ransom now I was alone. I stayed at the top holding on tight to both of them and watched O as though he were canoeing down the Rapids. I felt stranded, vulnerable and

108

very scared.

Jimmy remained at the bottom of the escalator, helplessly waiting for us to join him. O left the first suitcase with him and then got onto the 'up' escalator for the slow ascent to collect another. O continued like this until we had only the pram left with us at the top. When I finally stepped on to the 'down' escalator I felt I was flying. I had about four minutes to formulate my approach to Jimmy when I got to the bottom, but as soon as my feet landed on solid ground Jimmy made a dash for some turnstiles, where the masses became as flying fish, leaping and dodging death-defyingly over and through the rigid clockwork barriers.

After the brief comfort of the VIP lounge - black leather chairs and potted palms and glass cases displaying cigarettes and toys duty-free style - the tannoy announced our train and Jimmy sprang up from his seat. Struggling with the luggage we raced after him up a steep staircase and down a long tunnel which ended abruptly in a dark sea of heads and elbows, the familiar high-pitched cacophony of shouting Chinese, and the unmistakable melancholy wail of a train's siren. Unable to see the platform or the train, we pushed blindly through the hustling, pushing crowds towards where we felt instinctively there was an open door. As soon as he could see that we had clambered on board, Jimmy waved non-committally and was gone.

We grabbed four window seats at a table. Lace shawls were draped over the backs of the red-upholstered seats which matched the curtains. I turned away from the wall of jostling faces pressed at the window and saw that we were in the downstairs section of a two-storey train. On the half-way landing on the way to the WC stood an aspidistra on a lace crocheted mat next to a chair for the lady concierge.

Four sun-browned men sat at the table across the aisle. They nodded, with faint, polite smiles in our direction. I imagined they must be oil workers or miners from a wild, unforgiving outpost. With great concentration and care, one of the men - looking like a Chinese version of Charles Bronson - unwrapped a large soft white cloth over their table. Inside were pumpkin seeds which he counted into four equal piles. The tough, wiry men nibbled away the shells and ate the seeds for the next one and a half hours with great tenderness and respect, as though they were sacred delicacies. From time to time they smiled and waved at Hua Hua who looked away just in time.

Behind them was a large group of lady tourists in Burberry sun hats and lightweight raincoats. I thought they must be Korean: they were physically heavier than most Chinese women are and they seemed to aspire to the look of the middle-aged white American woman. Their organisational skills were impressive; each lady carried in a discreet Burberry waist-bag moist tissues, sweets, painkillers, travel games and ordinary tissues to double for the lavatory. Like the men in front of them they did not look out of the window throughout the journey and instead played games and made many trips to the WC, which, given its size, required a lot of organizational skills - most particularly for the tallest lady who wore a wide-brimmed straw hat decorated with artificial daffodils.

Chung Chung slept while Hua Hua remained awake and ate biscuits on our laps, bouncing about and knocking everything over. I watched the view outside, lush and flat to infinity, as it became by slow degrees more industrial as we neared Shanghai. The train was so intimate, it felt as though we were in the sitting room of the concierge who walked up and down the aisle, smiling and efficient in her dark, crisp uniform. The men fascinated me and the women fascinated me. I could have stayed on her train in this soothing people-watching limbo for much longer. However, we approached a twinkling Shanghai at magic hour and the comfort and quiet came to an end when our fellow travellers mobilised into a collective anxiety to prepare for an early exit.

Our new guide, Jenny Ling, found us as we squeezed through the turnstiles swept along by hundreds of boisterous Chinese travellers. She wrote her name on an old card in her pocket advertising 'Old Town Snack Palace and Old Town Hide Wind Pond', and on it she described herself as working for 'Shanghai Peace International Travel Service.' We ran behind her as she sprinted along the underpasses and wide walkways of the station to our waiting vanette and the big, bright, pulsating lights of Shanghai at dusk.

As night fell the vanette took us along the extraordinarily high city overpasses, in, amongst, and through the bright lights which gave the place a European feel; it felt to us like a combination of New York and Berlin. From the sickeningly high overpasses we could see into tiny apartments twenty floors high, their washing hanging out as usual precariously, and hundreds of feet in the air. We flew up into the bright lights of the flicker advertisements and past a huge hoarding alight with David Beckham drinking a Coke.

Jenny said she would tell us anything we wanted to know about Shanghai's history or tourist spots: the first important historical fact was, she said, that Shanghai girls are the most beautiful in China.

The "GrandNatioN Hotel" boasted an overwrought gold opulence in

Napoleonic-inspired style which oozed money, and a huge inner hall - an atrium, they described it - which continued as a gigantic empty space up to the gold, cupola'd roof. As I looked up, trying to make sense of the space, I wondered how much real estate value this awe-inspiring void was worth.

Once out of the lift on the seventeenth floor I understood the architecture; to get to our room we had to walk along a narrow balcony which fronted the doors of the rooms on all four sides of the huge void. O, Chung Chung and Hua Hua cheerfully strolled along the balcony with the bellboys and the bags. I was so scared that I flattened myself against the doors and edged sideways, slowly, hoping the doors opened inwards into the rooms.

Wednesday 28th March 2001, Grand Nation Hotel, Shanghai

The view of Shanghai from our room convinced me not to get nearer than four feet from the window. There seemed to be a very deep drop to ground level and we seemed to be far higher than seventeen floors. The buildings of Shanghai clustered together under a dull sky in random combinations of huge and ugly, and they looked to me like airbrushed architectural drawings of radio and television components standing on their ends; the thousands of dull, matte windows reflecting nothing, not even sky. The British Consulate was somewhere among them, but not open for visa applications until two p.m.

We met Jenny downstairs to check out and pay, leaving our luggage on a golden trolley decorated with Empire sphinxes and Baroque swags. O asked Jenny where she ate her lunch, because we would like to eat there too while we waited for the Consulate to open. She took us to Grandmother Dumpling's, an American-style self-service which served good value Chinese food to office workers and shop girls. The cheerful and plastic tables and the noise and bustle in there was very welcome after the crudely ostentatious GrandNatioN Hotel.

The British Consulate occupied a floor in a high, modern building which looked equivalently expensive, but a great deal less vulgar. We waited in a queue of young Chinese people who were anxious to take up the places in universities and language schools in Britain they had been offered. O was finally called to a clerk at a window. He returned to take more paperwork to the clerk. Through Jenny I tried to help a young man and his father answer questions on a form written in English. The father proudly told us that his son had been promised a place at a language school in Cambridge. He said that the British authorities doubted that he could support himself, but surely, the father remonstrated with me, they only have to look at me and see my gold rings and my fat stomach to know that I will finance my own son. He seemed to be having a hard time providing all the necessary paperwork. O was having a hard time too; he returned cross and frustrated now because the official refused to accept anything but cash in local currency for Hua Hua's visa.

O: 'Our adoption of Hua Hua was covered by a legal inter-country agreement which meant that he was now officially and legally our son, but he was not yet British, so he could travel to Britain with us only on a Chinese passport. For entry into Britain he required a visa from the British consulate. Despite the clarity of the agreement between the two countries and the strict laws put in place to support this agreement, a British official still felt it necessary to interview me from

112

behind bullet-proof glass in an interview room. She grilled me about my reasons for wanting to adopt from China, about my financial situation and even about my mother. It was as though she was carrying out her own homestudy to unilaterally authorise, or not, the Stockman family to adopt a second child. I was furious at her arrogance, and stung by the fact that she did not even ask about Hua Hua. I was sent back to the waiting room to actually wait for her decision to grant a visa; I wondered to what extent the officials took this game seriously, and whether they had ever refused a visa for a child adopted by British nationals?

Twenty minutes later I was called back in and informed that Hua Hua had been granted a visa. The official demanded £350.00 in local currency for it. I was stunned; it seemed a huge amount for a baby's visa, particularly compared with the one pound sterling which orphanages receive from the government per month, per child. Even airlines don't charge for infants, I thought angrily. The issue for us was not only a moral one: we had long ago run out of cash. I handed over my credit card. "No, Sir, we do not accept credit cards. We require cash in the national currency." The official would not negotiate; she refused credit cards, she refused a cheque and she refused to send us a bill to our UK address. She was adamant: no cash - no visa for the baby.

While Annabel waited with Hua Hua at the Carlton Hotel, Jenny, Chung Chung and I went to look for a bank. I had a few US dollars left because Hua Hua's adoption had cost us less than Ping Ping's and I still had Mr Yu's 'reparation' money. Jenny cashed her own money and with it bought my US dollars and I cashed our credit cards to make up the rest.'

O, Chung Chung and Jenny left me and Hua Hua to wait amongst the expensive soft furnishings at the Carlton Hotel while they left with all our credit cards on a mission to find a bank and a cash dispenser. The overstated understatement of the Carlton suggested to me that it would be frequented exclusively by big business people: the entrance lobby was so apparently understated that I had assumed at first we had walked into a large private bank.

Hua Hua and I sat beneath vast granite columns on a huge, plump, royal blue sofa watching a young, rather plain, Chinese woman and a late middle-aged Australian man working on each other with, I thought, a shocking cynicism. He wanted a girl to make him feel good. She wanted to get to the west on an easy ticket. He would not find it in the least bit difficult to smooth away Chinese bureaucracy and British visa cash requirements. The young woman managed, in between tiny sips of espresso and coquettish nibbles of bite-sized almond amaretti, to show a

113

tremendous interest in this unappealing man with his grinning, liver spots, flushed complexion and fat, pink hands.

We watched the waitresses in pseudo traditional silk dresses, split provocatively to the knee, serve them minimalist coffee and strong drinks. When a very good-looking waitress delivered my coffee on a small tray with a royal blue flower in a small glass vase, green sugar and pink Italian biscuits I began to feel nervous. She wasn't wearing the thick skin-coloured hose so popular with the staff in the tourist hotels we were used to, and she was so exquisite she did not even register Hua Hua's presence on the sofa; she might expect a big tip, I speculated anxiously. When Hua Hua had sucked his way through our 'complimentary' sweet biscuits the discreet waitresses again didn't seem to notice that he had been drooling a mixture of dribble and amaretto crumbs across the vast expanse of royal blue upholstery. I felt obliged, for their sake, to try to appear at my ease while I made my designer cup of very expensive coffee last as long as I reasonably could.

O, Chung Chung and Jenny returned triumphant, having visited a number of cash dispensers in Shanghai. O, now feeling - relatively - richer and in great need of a real coffee, ordered for all of us. We sipped and munched in silence, dumbfounded by the scale of money we found ourselves sitting in. The couple exchanging temptations and whispers about visas had gone without my noticing. I struggled to sit upright amongst the soft, elephantine creases of the sofa; like Hua Hua, I was almost asleep.

We waited in the vanette while O collected and paid in cash for Hua Hua's visa at the British Consulate. I asked Jenny about her plans for the future: Did she want to visit the west? "Yes," she said, "very much," but she is a government worker living with her mother and she needs to prove that she has a good life to return to; owning a car for example would convince the authorities that she would not try to stay in the west. I thought about the young woman in the Carlton Hotel: I bet she didn't have a car either, nor would all those young people in the queue for visas at the Consulate.

We continued on in the vanette to Shanghai Zoo, collecting our luggage from the GrandNatioN Hotel on the way. The Zoo was out of town en route to the airport and the weather was fine. It seemed perfect to spend a carefree afternoon devoted to Chung Chung's serious passion for animals. Jenny offered, without enthusiasm, to join us in our gentle wanderings, muttering about being exhausted from a Spanish group of adopters she took around Shanghai a few days ago. We insisted she stay and rest, we would be fine; in fact we were happy to shake her off. I found her unimaginative and painfully conventional, with her lipstick and Shanghai

114

sophistication. She smiled, looking immensely relieved and straightaway she curled up, with her feet on the dashboard and her head on her knees and went to sleep. Unabashed, the driver dug into his pockets for matches, lit a cigarette, slid his seat back and propped his feet up onto his open window. He looked as though he was settling in for a long wait.

The driver knew about Shanghai Zoo, but didn't have the English to tell us. Jenny did have the English, but didn't think to tell us that the Zoo occupied a huge expanse of land and that we needed to buy a map to avoid becoming lost in it. After an hour and a half of trudging, circling, and observing wistfully that we were being regularly overtaken by the same motorised cart pulling wagons full of smiling people, we found the Giant Panda munching on bamboo and large bricks of compressed nutrients. Like the few animals we had managed to find - despite the zoo's quota of over two thousand animals and birds - the panda looked very healthy and very well cared for.

While we politely jostled for space at the window to see the panda, the animal watched us from the back of the large, highly polished glass, chrome and tile house. He seemed to smile, disinterestedly, regarding without judgement and eating continually, while humanity fought for a space for a photo opportunity in front of his window.

Finally hungry, thirsty and dusty, and saturated with anything to do with zoos, we guessed our way towards the exit by the set of the sun and found Jenny and the driver fast asleep in the vanette across the road in the car park. We were also saturated with the irrelevant help that Jenny had to offer. We asked to be driven direct to the airport. It was still only four-thirty p.m. and our plane was due to take off at eleven p.m., but the prospect of a long wait at an airport perversely conjured in us images of the joy and release of independence and an opportunity for a long, leisurely supper. The idea of being free and unattended, and finally together as a family, gave us a new energy. Jenny and the driver didn't hesitate. The vanette hurtled down the short stretch of freeway to the airport. We found ourselves thirty minutes later, having shrugged off the grateful Jenny, standing in the newest, largest, and most recently brushed-chrome contemporary architectural concept that we had so far been in. And we were completely alone.

115

Thursday 29th March 2001, BA flight Paris - London

Shanghai Airport was staggering, as vast as two football pitches, fantastically clean, halogen lit and totally, eerily empty. We floated around this matte chrome cathedral virtually alone for over six hours. The shops and the two restaurants closed early and we missed our anticipated celebratory supper. Instead we experimented with the sliding doors, we slid on the aluminium floors, we sat on all the newfangled seating, and we did somersaults on the chrome handrails. This was a surreal decompression, nocturnal and silent.

'We took off late last night. Hua Hua- who now has a chest infection- was unstoppable and played musical chairs for thirteen hours. O remained awake looking after him. Chung Chung, thankfully, slept. I dozed, in patches, nightmarishly re-living events, and awoke staring into the dark of the stale airborne dormitory, agonising about Ping Ping. Again, the old-hand Chinese travellers slept across the seats with their stockinged feet propped on the armrests, toes in the aisles. In the air-conditioned quiet the sound of sleep was oddly reassuring.'

We arrived in Paris at four-thirty a.m. French time and caught the seven a.m. BA flight to London. As we neared the top of the rickety steps onto the aircraft, grubby, sweaty, hungry and disoriented I felt a surge of energy as a sensation of home appeared to me like a vision. The sun was rising behind the little plane. The neat and comfortingly effeminate flight attendant smiled at us. "Welcome aboard, have a nice journey!" Instant, sweet recognition of the modulation of sounds this stranger made restored me and filled me with gratitude. He was taking us all home. I could have embraced him.

Neale kissed me as we came out into the Arrivals area at Heathrow. We were late after a series of interviews with immigration officials and we were carrying only hand luggage. (Our luggage had not been loaded onto the plane in Paris.) He looked puzzled, concerned. He gave Hua Hua a big smile. Hua Hua looked away, intrigued. Outside the airport the sun was still rising and opening into a cloud-streaked canopy of pink haze. We moved off to the minivan and climbed back into our lives amongst the monkey wrenches, tarpaulins and scattered petrol receipts.

Hua Hua sat on my lap as the minivan crawled in the morning rush hour conveyer belt. London was discreetly sunny and a gentle layer of grime subdued any colour. I gazed like a stranger at the suburban streets and miniature conurbations; the front gardens, the pavements, the traffic

116

junctions, the little parks and the corner shops. It was all so different, so small, so...silent, and so empty. This big city, London, seemed to be uninhabited, private, almost secretive. The few people walking to work moved differently and they were shaped differently. They walked in ones and twos instead of hundreds. There were solitary bicycles. The cars were not hooting. There was no washing hanging.

Neale cheerfully called back to us from the drivers' seat. "Pleased to be home?" "Yes!" we called back, struggling to remain awake. "Can't hear you!", "*Yes!*" we called louder. Chung Chung had fallen asleep on O's lap. She had been so stoical, so patient and so good all through our Chinese adventure.

While we were away winter had become spring.

EPILOGUE

Hua Hua would not look anyone in the eye for a long time and he would not accept to be looked at; he merely turned away, averting his eyes to the floor or to me. Sometimes he seemed quite agitated when men tried to make contact with him and I had to reassure him by holding him tight.

After a few days with us at home Hua Hua rediscovered his confidence and took up shouting and yelling. This was a habit he had learnt at Fuyang orphanage and he liked it. The noise worked very well with us so he continued to shout for comfort and food. He still does. Chung Chung found the noise difficult and still does. He broke things, and this was difficult, too. People reminded us that he was a boy; our adjustment to Hua Hua was slow and gradual, nevertheless we all delighted in him, and laughed at his clowning and sweetness.

O, meanwhile was back in the office dealing with various horrors that had accumulated while we were away. Nevertheless he found time in the first few days of our return to e-mail our friends on the Ping Jiang orphanage website and describe what had happened in China. He requested urgently that Ping Ping's situation be made known should someone feel able to adopt him. O received many sympathetic responses and after a week he had two positive replies asking more about Ping Ping. One of them was from Deidre Dudley who was the programme director for Cambodia, China, Vietnam, Kazakhstan and the Ukraine for an American adoption agency. She and her husband Rick, a Marine Chemist, had two of their own children - 'bio' in adoption jargon - and had adopted seven girls from Asia, many of them apparently with special needs. Deidre offered to look for parents for Ping Ping. A week later Deidre sent word to O that she and her husband had discussed the possibility of adopting Ping Ping themselves and had decided that this was what they wanted to do.

O and Deidre continued to communicate by e-mail, discussing Ping Ping's condition, the therapy he would need and how best to proceed with the Dudley's application for him discreetly, though again unusually, requesting the CCAA for him by name.

Deidre sent updates on their progress and preparations for Ping Ping. They built an addition onto their house because, she wrote," since he is a boy, coming to a house full of girls, we thought he should have his own room." Her commitment and excitement and her sense of mission gave me tremendous comfort.

Unexpectedly, only eight months after Deidre had first contacted O, the

CCAA sent her Ping Ping's referral documents for signing, followed quickly by her permission to travel to collect him. Deidre e-mailed us from Changsha on the ninth of November 2001;

"Dear Olivier and Annabel

We have Ping Ping and he is adorable!!
We just thank you so much for telling us of Brett Ping Jiang. I am sure that he was meant to be our son and it was just to occur by way of your family. I am sorry that you had to experience the sadness of leaving him in China, but I can only say that it was part of a bigger plan than we can know! You have your wonderful son and we have ours and all is well for all now. I hope our families will always be bonded by this experience and that you will visit sometime to meet Ping Ping a second time!! He is a doll!!!

God Bless you all!

Deidre, mom to Brett Ping Jiang, the cutest little boy in the world!!"

Ten days later Deidre e-mailed O from Baton Rouge. "Brett is so very affectionate and the girls just love him." I called her on the telephone for the first time; I wanted her to know how grateful I was, and comforted, relieved...reprieved. Her voice was warm, singing, and she giggled. I could feel her clarity and sense. She described the man who was with Ping Ping when she first walked into the hotel room. He said he was the Director and Ping Ping's carer. It wasn't Mr Yu. When she asked him about Ping Ping's health the man insisted that there was nothing wrong with Ping Ping, that he had never had seizures and that he had never been on medication. Those raw feelings of confusion and betrayal swirled around again: Deidre's soothing voice reminded me Ping Ping was safe now. "Best not to think about it too much: he's here now and he's our baby boy!" she said, "and he's gonna be fine with us!"

We continued to keep in touch and sent cards and presents on his birthday and at Christmas. Deidre e-mailed regularly about his progress. When Ping Ping was three Deidre told us that he was improving: "I think God is working a miracle in this little boy and the doctors just can't admit it yet. He is doing so well, still not walking independently, but he can beat me across the room crawling when he wants to. He plays chase with the girls around the couch in the living room and laughs and laughs until he falls over! He is starting to 'sing' to music and definitely knows when you tell him "NO!" He hides his face and hopes that you will forget! He is such a

119

sweet spirit!"

I wrote to Deidre to ask her if she would allow me to include her e-mails in this book. She replied,

"I will share something that I don't think I have shared with you before. When we travelled for Brett, I knew he was delayed and his diagnosis/prognosis was very unclear, but I was optimistic that when I arrived I would find a little boy that was not as badly off as everyone had thought. However when I saw him the first time, and during the first week there, I knew he was very involved and that he was not going to be completely OK just with a lot of love. I woke many times during the night praying for direction. I had seven other children at home and I was scared! I even contemplated leaving him too, but my wonderful friend Kevin who travelled with me assured me that I MUST take him out of there. I prayed and was given peace by telling myself that if he was too involved and we couldn't take care of him, I could always find him another home. I decided that perhaps God had sent me to get him, because I knew how to and I could afford it. Maybe this was the part I was to play in his life. Even after arriving back home there were times I was so tired and frightened that I had taken on more than I could handle. It was such a tumultuous time, with so many emotions. I prayed day and night and finally God showed me that we were so in love with him and he with us and that we were the perfect family for him.

I am so happy to have Brett and all the things I said about loving him were absolutely true, but I just didn't tell the whole story at the time. It would not have served anyone well at the time."

**"We inherit what is natural,
but culture can come only through education."**

François Truffaut

ACKNOWLEDGEMENTS

We would like to express our admiration and deep gratitude to the Dudley family in Baton Rouge, USA for their unconditional love for Brett Ping Jiang.

Our great thanks to Lida (Dong Wenna) who spoke for us so passionately, to the CCAA who listened so patiently, and to Don and Wendi Harris for posting Ping Ping's SOS to 8,000 adoptive families, leading to Ping Ping's adoption with the Dudleys.

Many thanks for help with translations to Hing Tsang and Tina and Harry Ho, and for support to Anna Black, Neale Brown, Camilla Connell, Childlink, Janet Hammond, Joanna Hands, Maryvonne Gervais de Lafond, Christine Goodwin, Christine Manning and Emerald-jane Turner.

Thanks, too, to Sheila Coe for her reading of the early draft and to Chung Chung's Old Friend Suzanne Adams for her help with Spelling, Grammar and Rules of Thumb...

A month after our trip to China the CCAA initiated a new rule which requires orphanages to arrange for matched babies to be examined by a doctor at a hospital a week prior to their adoption. The resulting medical report then forms part of the legal adoption document.

NOTES

O - Olivier Stockman my husband. We live and work with a group of people in warehouses in Rotherhithe, London, making films

Chung Chung - Amandine Chung Chung Elisebeth Jiang Yan (Blazing River) Stockman. Born 12.04.97 near Ping Jiang town, Hunan. Adopted 20.04.98 Changsha and Yue Yang, Hunan Province, China

Ping Ping - Jiang Xiao Hu (Little Tiger River), born 6.04.2000, near Ping Jiang town, Hunan

Ping Jiang - The small village very close to a river where Chung Chung and Ping Ping's orphanage is. Ping means level, equal or gentle, Jiang means River (the village wishes the river not to swell). All the orphanage children share the family name 'Jiang'

Department of Health - The adoption section through which all international adoptions are finally approved, processed and sent overseas to equivalent government departments. Christine Manning was our contact there

Referral papers - The official offer from the Chinese authorities (the CCAA) of a child for adoption, with medical report and photograph

Neale and the Squirrel van - the studio manager, caterer, transport director, plumber, projectionist, tour guide, etc etc

CCAA - China Centre for Adoption Affairs in Beijing, the counterpart government office

Yu Yong Gao - Mr Yu, the Director of Ping Jiang Social Welfare Institute, the orphanage

Hing Tsang - A Chinese film-maker friend, fluent in many languages, born in London

Dragon Boy - The Chinese sign of the Zodiac considered to be the most desirable, for it encapsulates the best aspects of all the other signs. Boys have traditionally been more admired than girls in China

Childlink - The Childlink Adoption Society provided a social worker to interview us over eight weeks to prepare a report (a 'Homestudy') on our fitness to adopt. Their panel's 'Approval' was passed to our local council adoption section as a recommendation to the council's panel.

Southwark - the London Borough of Southwark approved the adoption and passed their recommendation on to the Department of Health Inspector in the adoption section

BLAS - The Bridge of Love Adoption Service. A government authorised travel agency which arranges travel, accommodation and guide interpreters for the adoption process in China

Lida, Stella, Jessie, Jenny, Jimmy, Lesley, Doris. The Chinese choose new names (mainly English) for themselves for western consumption

The Tattooed man - in the past those who had gone to prison were branded with their crime as a lifelong punishment

Zhong Ping - the girl who first cared for Chung Chung at Pingjiang and cried when she had to hand her over to us

Cerebral Palsy - the impairment of muscular function and weakness of the limbs, caused by damage to the brain before or during birth

Maryvonne - O's stepmother in Paris

Christine - Christine Edzard Goodwin who lives and works with us in the studios. She is the children's guardian

Hua Hua - Louis Hua Hua Buster Jijun Stockman. Born 02.01. 2000 near Fuyang town, Zhejiang Province. Left on the doorstep of a farmer. Adopted 23.03.01, Hangzhou, Zhejiang, China